LEADING
CHANGE
in the Public Sector

Practical strategies for moving
efforts forward in government

PATRICK K. CHAPMAN

Nordic Press
New York, NY

First Edition: April 2011

The Nordic Press name and logo are trademarks of the Nordic
Book Group. All other third-party names and trademarks are
copyrighted by their respective organization.

ISBN-10: 0-615-46139-5
ISBN-13: 978-0-615-46139-7

To
William Carleton
and
Jonathan Moore

Too much th sut
is "policy" not
= "process"

"what" not "how"

Contents

Acknowledgements

The author wishes to express his gratitude to his family for their enduring support. Deepest gratitude is also extended to Jonathan Moore and William Carleton for demonstrating everyday what it means to be passionate about driving value, focused on quality, and making an impact. The author also wishes extend a special thank you to Scott McIntyre, Peter Raymond, and the men and women of his professional services firm for their leadership, guidance, and exceptional service delivery support.

For those working in or supporting government organizations, the terms 'effective' and 'government' often feel further apart than any two words ever uttered. In many public sector organizations, the landscape of government employees and contractors resembles a cycle of hope and desperation rivaled only by those visiting the Las Vegas strip. New employees and fresh consultants begin with a positive attitude, ready to create change, increase efficiency, or improve services. These idealistic individuals eventually meet the realities of many government cultures - one where few are willing to make a decision, everyone needs to have a say, a single dissenter can kill anything, and a management requiring 'another study' before acting.

Despite what may appear to be a fairly bleak picture, the truth is effective government is possible, but a large part of the solution for individuals tasked with moving efforts forward lies in this: Not trying to fix government's largest problems at the same time. Before most people can move anything forward in organizations that evolved over decades to be what they are today, they must accept that many of the biggest challenges plaguing their organizations are simply intractable. Separate books could and have been written about why this is. Countless studies have pointed to a lack of market driven pressures driving increased efficiency, an absence of meaningful accountability for organizations and individuals, or the declining value of civil service careers relative to private sector opportunities. Solving these and other issues are often purposely or inadvertently put on the critical path of major initiatives or projects, ultimately dooming the efforts. The bottom line is that individuals working in or supporting government organizations must embrace ways to be productive despite the realities of their environment.

Is the basic concept of avoiding the biggest issues enough to make government initiatives or projects successful? Of course the traditional components of success are still required including well defined objectives, a thoughtful approach, consistent execution, appropriately skilled resources, and others. However, while these components alone are often enough in commercial organizations, they are usually not sufficient to ensure success in a government culture. By examining successful and failed efforts in government organizations, a set of interrelated commonalities emerge that most successful efforts possess and failed ones lack; basic techniques focused on enabling progress without requiring individuals to first fix everything that inhibits it.

Fundamentally, these techniques are based largely on a single over-arching premise: Incremental progression is a significantly superior approach in cultures that are adverse to change and possess high levels of internal politics. The larger or more sudden proposed progress is within these organizations, the lower the chance of success. Efforts built on incremental progress allow an organization to consume change at a pace that does not trigger a predictable series of obstacles from its resources and culture.

These techniques also require in many ways a redefinition of success. The achievement of smaller goals; progress towards rather than reaching a destination; and outcomes measured over longer periods of time. The realities of the environment dictate this redefinition. The concepts contained within this book support their achievement. To further illustrate the need and value of specific techniques, let's briefly examine the traditional elements that support success in the private sector versus the public sector.

The Traditional Equation

If you examine projects or initiatives in the private sector, the foundation for success is generally constructed through a combination of strong subject matter expertise and strong project management. Appropriate subject matter expertise enables good definition of objectives, solid solution design, and the ability to course correct as necessary during implementation. Strong project management capability shepherds an effort through appropriate planning and execution monitoring.

Unsuccessful efforts in the private sector typically lack one or both of these key components. Poor subject matter expertise translates into poor solutions and little or no course correction. Poor project management often translates into delays or budget overruns. Private sector initiatives may fail for other reasons as well, but almost never succeed without these elements.

Other elements including change management activities such as stakeholder communication are important but typically act as facilitators or accelerators to an effort. When the goal in a private sector organization is to move a boulder up a hill, people are given the opportunity to move with it, but the boulder will move even if those who won't ultimately get rolled over by it.

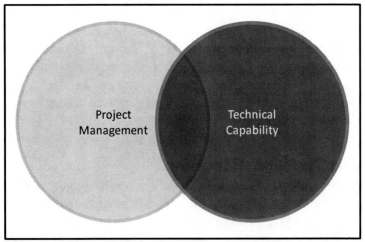

Figure 1: The traditional foundation for successful initiatives in the private sector.

The Public Sector Equation

In a public sector organization, not only may some individuals who decide not to move stop the boulder, many may be actively or even successfully pushing against it. Dealing with this common reality means individuals must fully leverage the tools of *public sector change management* in addition to the traditional components of strong subject matter expertise and project management.

The realities of the public sector clearly require a different type of change management; a set of techniques that go beyond typical change mechanisms such as executive sponsorship, communications, and training. Public sector change techniques designed to operate within the typical environments of government organizations supplement traditional change management activities to further facilitate and drive efforts forward.

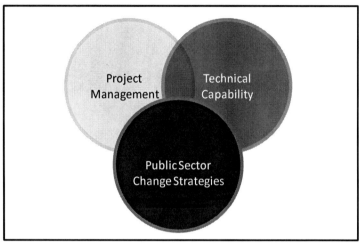

Figure 2: Public Sector initiatives often require specialized change strategies in addition to the traditional components.

To support a better understanding of these techniques, this book consists of two major segments. The first segment, encompassing sections 1-3, provides background for the techniques including what makes public sector organizations different; what drives change in government; and a summary of traditional change management levers. The second segment, comprising the remaining sections, describes a number of change management strategies that have proven particularly effective in the public sector. Individuals who leverage some or all of these techniques in combination with traditional project and operational approaches will hopefully find that working with, rather than trying to change, the reality in which they operate results in greater levels of success and the personal satisfaction associated with making a real difference.

The Realities of the Public Sector

Government environments are often equated simply with bureaucracy – obscure forms, multiple approval cycles, layers of policy, etc. The reality for those who must operate within these environments is actually significantly more challenging than those who must interface with it. These characteristics often do exist, but are frequently layered into an organization that simultaneously lacks formal approval chains for many decisions, maintains few documented and up to date processes, and possesses little or no consistency in the application of policies across the organization. What many in government find are organizations that possess varying degrees of many common characteristics, significantly inhibiting an individual's ability to move projects and initiatives forward.

The attributes summarized in this section are not meant to represent an exhaustive examination of the characteristics of government cultures. They do however clearly illustrate the need for special techniques to enable progress.

1

High Levels of Decentralization

Most major federal organizations maintain responsibility for a highly diverse and often disparate set of missions. Their evolution has occurred over decades, with a general direction of consolidation into larger departments representing a portfolio of related services or goals. Under the hood, these departments maintain a wide range of tightly and loosely coupled operating models and in some cases, almost no relationship below the congressional funding level.

The US Department of Energy (DOE) represents a great example of this underlying diversification. DOE encompasses research and science programs including fossil, renewable, and nuclear energy; environmental remediation and clean up organizations; regulatory responsibilities; nuclear weapons security; power marketing administrations; and dozens of technology labs and centers. Within each of these organizations lies a broad array of sub-organizations resulting in more than 1,000 distinct groups within the department. Similar to DOE, virtually all major departments and agencies across the federal government possess substantial numbers and layers of formal sub-organizations which occasionally maintain overlapping, and even competing, missions and functions. Mechanisms for ongoing coordination between these groups usually exist outside the formal organizational structure, frequently manifesting themselves as cross-organizational working groups or committees.

The significance and impact of this diversity is often overlooked when consultants and others advise the government to act more like the private sector. From a diversity of product, service, and focus perspective, most of today's larger public sector institutions are closer akin to very large global conglomerates rather than more singularly focused corporations. Even in the private sector, conglomerates often forgo coordination beyond strategy and instead rely on a more decentralized or localized management approach similar to that adopted by most large public sector institutions. In essence, public sector organizations do organize themselves at the highest levels somewhat like their closest private sector equivalents - what they lack however is the incredibly powerful profit motive that no 'acting like' can replace.

Shared services, a common private sector approach whereby a centralized group provides supporting services across some or all organizational units, remains a difficult concept to successfully implement in government. As public sector organizations react to various pressures to increase effectiveness or efficiency stemming from events such as budget cuts or increased oversight, the desire to consolidate and centralize certain activities becomes more attractive. However, even assessing the feasibility of this often requires the heavy use of public sector change management techniques described in this book to accomplish successfully.

A common issue for shared services groups in the public sector and one that perpetuates decentralization for many functions is a general lack of satisfaction with the level of service they provide. The root cause for the lack of satisfaction is often a combination of factors including regulatory constraints beyond the control of the services organization, poorly structured contracts for support, a lack of effective communication by all parties, or simply a lack of customer-oriented service techniques and supporting technologies. The dissatisfaction, when not addressed, spurs further decentralization over time and breeds resistance to centralized services models when in reality a variety of more straightforward enhancements would allow the organization to enjoy the efficiencies of centralization without a reduction in effectiveness. Within these shared services organizations lies the greatest opportunity for public sector organizations to 'act' like their private sector equivalents.

2

A Lack of Decision-Making Structures

The foundational activity for getting anything done in organizations is decision-making. Whether by an executive, committee, or simply a willing individual, the very basis for moving things forward is a made decision. Within government organizations, decision-making typically exists at three basic levels, based on the general reach and impact of a given decision. At the bottom level, the decision-makers are usually well-defined for low-level needs such as the approval of a travel request or invoice payment. At the top, the organization's most strategic decisions, often those for which the organization was created to make, are also typically well defined in the form of a formal commission or one or more specific senior executive level positions. Areas such as rule-making or fining a business are typically more thoroughly vetted based on reach and impact and may have been refined over time by various lobbying organizations, special interest groups, and lawsuits.

The vast middle of the decision framework in government however often remains undefined where decisions about internal investments, whether to initiate a project, or how to accomplish sub-objectives are left to more informal mechanisms to address. A single assertive individual may 'call the ball' and simply make a decision although many actions simply happen (or don't) based on whether enough inertia exists behind something. Because so many decisions fall into this middle area, the lack of decision-making is often enough to fully stall otherwise constructive opportunities for improvement.

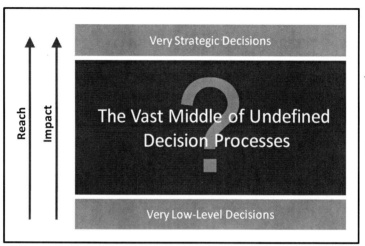

Figure 3: The decision-making gap commonly existing in many public sector organizations.

Decision-making vacuums in government are frequently filled by singular loud personalities or very passionate participants. If the individual is promoting healthy paths, the outcomes work well for the organization. However, when these individuals back ideas or decisions that lead an organization down the wrong path, few mechanisms typically exist to naturally course correct. Ultimately it may take years and millions of dollars to get an organization or project back on a good track.

Many organizations attempt to close the vacuum with some type of 'governance' structure or group involving management from one or more organizations. Unfortunately these groups are often either never given real authority or simply fail to truly exercise their authority based on the membership's appetite for accepting the natural risk that accompanies a decision.

For individuals working in these environments, the ubiquitous lack of decision-making can start to create a highly jaundiced attitude about what is truly possible in the environment. The repeated introduction of new initiatives followed by a lack of decisions to implement real changes starts to make an individual feel like Charlie Brown being asked to kick the ball they inevitably know Lucy is going to pull. Trust diminishes followed often by the will to genuinely try.

3

Few Well-Defined Processes

Another common characteristic of government organizations is that a significant number of operational processes are not formally contemplated, designed, and documented. Process documentation may exist, perhaps in significant volume, but this documentation often consists more of policy than process - what one must do rather than how one does it. Detailed process documentation, when it does exist, is also often significantly out of date.

A lack of consistent and well-defined processes has an enormous impact on an organization's culture as well as its performance. Without good processes, the organization lacks fundamental ways to track activities that need to get done until they actually get done, ways to measure volume, gauge performance, route work, or know what stage any particular matter is in. In smaller organizations with lower volumes of activity the lack of processes merely results in cracks that are easily crossed by competent staff. But in bigger organizations or those with heavier work volume, these cracks stretch open to become gaping chasms into which a significant amount of activity falls. The result is a process that feels to many like a game of 'chutes and ladders' where sometimes, almost randomly, steps are repeated, introduced, or out of order based on who's doing it and whether people did what they were supposed to do.

When many people think of defined processes, they imagine workflow diagrams showing steps as boxes with arrows between them. Unfortunately this is where many process definition or improvement efforts end. The reality is this is only the first step. Today virtually *all* real and operational office processes are designed and implemented in software. If the process isn't implemented in and driven by a system, the process is rarely followed and few if any benefits of the defined process are realized. This reality is often lost on external consultants who work with public sector organizations to define on paper very good processes but fail to adequately consider how and in what systems or tools the processes are actually implemented. Repeated documentation-only efforts lead to the belief over time that 'documented processes' aren't very useful and simply occupy shelf space.

When the documented and software-driven processes are absent, an organization's systems typically provide little benefit beyond information capture and simple reporting. Because one of the primary goals of software is to support business processes, the absence of defined processes during development or integration translates into the implementation of a system that merely captures data or documents in simple forms. Nothing is truly automated because there was nothing defined to automate. In the end, because the systems were not developed to handle workflow, the system's very existence and use now actually inhibits the future ability to automate processes.

4

Heavy Use of
Working Groups

High levels of decentralization combined with a strong desire for inclusiveness in the public sector gives rise to a large number of cross-organization working groups dedicated to addressing various issues or opportunities. These groups, typically numbering between eight and twenty people, meet periodically to address a wide variety of short and longer term topics. In many public sector organizations working groups act as the main contemplating mechanism focused on the 'vast middle' of the decision-making process.

The diverse and cross-cutting nature of public sector working groups often drives a common profile of participants, each with their own needs or agendas which occasionally conflict with the working groups over-arching goals. For example, a large segment of the working group may not participate in any meaningful way, another segment may participate only when specifically engaged, a few may be actively working against the goals of the group, and a small segment of vested individuals pulls everyone else along.

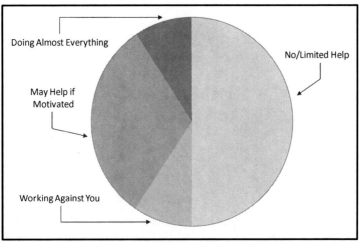

Figure 4: A frequent distribution of motivation/participation in cross-organizational working groups.

In addition, the natural disconnect between a working group and the formal organizations which directly manage funding and activity often results in the investment of substantial time and energy in the development of proposed ideas and solutions which are never adopted or implemented. This lack of formal authority coupled with the working group's inherent contemplative approach and loose structure, results in many groups becoming stuck in the production of information as opposed to engaging in meaningful action. So often is this cycle repeated that many working group efforts include a start-up period consisting of a review of previous internal and external efforts focused on the same problem. In one government organization for example, a list was recently compiled for a working group summarizing all of the documents and reports analyzing the organization's human capital approaches and performance. Covering the period of 1995 to late 2010, the list contained fifty-six distinct internal and external review efforts.

In some government cultures, inclusiveness within working groups is taken to such an extreme that the working group is rendered almost useless by its desire to incorporate every possible viewpoint and opinion on a given subject. Beyond the time investment, the more significant impact of total inclusion is that ideas, good ideas, are often watered down or rejected by the group in order to accommodate a minority of disagreement. The result is the removal of true meaning and impact from group recommendations to the organization's leadership. One working group in a federal organization for example had determined after months of meeting the need to make specific changes to its quality assurance functions. After debate with a minority of dissent the recommendation was changed from specific changes to 'changes to be 'agreed upon'. After that recommendation went through a round of leadership review and concurrence, the final recommendation simply stated that quality assurance 'could be improved'.

Regardless of the exact mix of working group personalities, their lack of real authority, or high levels of inclusiveness, individuals who wish to be successful in getting things done within a federal culture must learn how to effectively drive progress through the working group model.

5

A Substantial Focus
on Compliance

Government activities are driven by a complex web of laws and oversight mechanisms that direct agencies to engage in specific functions to accomplish their missions. From Congressional acts to Office of Management and Budget (OMB) circulars to external audits, a typical government organization's activities are authorized, refined, mandated, clarified, contradicted, and directed by multiple governing bodies.

To ensure agencies are executing their missions consistent with their requirements and acting in the best interest of their stakeholders and taxpayers, additional layers of internal and external oversight and control mechanisms exist. These mechanisms drive a substantial amount of organizational activity designed simply to document that an agency is doing what it's supposed to be doing. In some government organizations, the existence of entire departments is based on the need to provide evidence and information to other groups based on a law or an OMB requirement to collect and report the information.

The intention of the oversight bodies that provide the guidance or require the documentation is to drive some kind of additional value. They're looking for a positive result such as better decision-making, increased efficiency, or reduced duplication of effort or investments. For example OMB, which provides substantial guidance to federal organizations requires those organizations to plan for and review investments in their major systems. OMB's objective is to get organizations to actively engage in appropriate governance and planning. A laudable goal. Their approach to accomplishing this however is to require a significant amount of documentation illustrating the assessment of options, required investment levels over time, major risks, and other investment attributes.

Unfortunately more effort is frequently put into simply creating the documentation to satisfy this requirement than into using the guidance to drive value. In many public sector organizations, millions of dollars are spent developing this documentation for OMB despite the fact that it's not actually tied into their real investment consideration activities. In many cases, the OMB paperwork is developed after the acquisitions process is well underway or after a decision has already been made in which case the paperwork is perfunctory. In addition, because the documentation can be voluminous, additional efforts are often frequently engaged in to summarize the documentation into executive briefings, resulting in resources expended to summarize the contents of a document which served little or no organizational benefit to begin with.

When multiplied across all of a government organization's functions and activities, the sheer level of time and resources expended simply to comply with the documentation demands of oversight mechanisms represents an enormous ongoing investment. Unfortunately much of this investment frequently fails to translate into real or material organizational value.

6

Longer Cycle Times

Often an agency's consensus-oriented culture, compliance requirements, and other factors translates into significantly longer cycle times for any effort, large or small. The sources or root causes for these delays within the public sector are many and varied. In some cases, an organization may circulate even simple documents or draft emails for review and concurrence by a large number of internal and external personnel. In other cases, items simply wait for a decision that one or more leaders are reluctant to make.

Many activities and efforts also become bogged down by the extra steps embedded in the process to comply with laws or other regulations. Even simple exchanges of information or using a software utility to facilitate an effort may create months of delays to comply with a variety of regulations and required security and compliance requirements. In other cases, it's simply the re-submission of lost requests that can drag out an activity cycle. As described in chapter three, a lack of automation and workflow can result in delays and iterative submissions representing, for all intents and purposes, part of the standard process.

Large scale efforts, with their multiple work streams, are often significantly impacted by cycle time issues. These efforts often fall far behind schedule over time due to plans that failed to appropriately build in how long it truly takes in the public sector to successfully execute even simple tasks, such as providing building access to a temporary worker or getting approval to share information, which can take weeks or sometimes months. These often hidden 'time-sucks' are difficult to fully plan for resulting in the frequent development of project or activity schedules that appear appropriate but prove unrealistic (or when realistic appear to be giving way too much time to simple activities). How long will it take to interview a department head? Many schedules for example will include one to three days of time for the activity; but it might take three days just to go through review and approval of the invite message. Like death by a thousand small cuts, efforts often fall continuously further behind over time.

These cycle time issues represent a significant risk to any change effort because the basic nature of organizations dictates that the longer something takes to accomplish, the greater the risk it will get derailed before it's completed.

7

Duplicative Technologies

Another characteristic of many government organizations is the level of duplication in technologies deployed to address the same technical or business problems. There are a number of reasons for this, including the decentralized nature of organizations which often focus specifically on addressing their own immediate needs. It is common for government organizations to possess multiple systems to address the same function such as people directories, asset management systems, and even e-mail systems.

While decentralization is one driver for technical duplication, another is the basic desire for information control, and the common struggle between centralized functional organizations and decentralized programmatic organizations. Playing out across the government landscape is an on-going tug-of-war between 'headquarters' and the field' within each organization for control of spending and activity direction. Each individual office or department's information, such as spending and performance data represent ammunition in this war and group-specific systems to secure and control this information are considered vital for maintaining control.

The duplicative systems and their corresponding lack of centralized information create enormous difficulty for managers and others who seek visibility across multiple organizations for the purposes of improved management or building a business case for change. Instead, visibility is achieved through frequent 'data calls' to sub-organizations for updates or information. The basis for such requests stem from a variety of internal sources as well as outside an agency from organizations such as OMB. These requests often manifest themselves as a formatted spreadsheet template requiring population with information no one may have ever collected and are frequently due back in an expedited timeframe. The data calls themselves are also often duplicated as similar information is collected for different purposes. At one organization for example, three data calls were received the same week asking the leadership to classify what roles people played; one for OMB, one for an agency-wide working group, and a third for a consulting study focused on identifying efficiencies. Each data call requested a different categorization and methodology for its population.

It's often said that information is power. For change efforts the frequent foundation for making a powerful case for change is the use of quantitative data, which is viewed as more compelling than anecdotal evidence. The existence of duplicative systems with different data and information types and perhaps more importantly, system owners with reluctance to hand over large sets of raw data make the development of concrete cases for change that much more difficult to create.

8

Limited Organizational Visibility

The government's many and varied oversight mechanisms create what can appear to be a seemingly continuous review of any given public sector organization's activities, often manifesting themselves as audits from internal organizations such as an agency's Inspector General's office as well as external sources such as the Government Accountability Office (GAO). The traditional approach for these organizations is to collect information through documentation review and interviews, develop findings, and issue an often publicly available report. The frequent use of audits and related performance measurement approaches have resulted in generating considerable defensiveness on the part of the target organizations over time which has inhibited their willingness to provide visibility into their activities and performance. With a lack of reward mechanisms for positive findings, the public nature of most audit or review findings, and their frequency, few if any natural incentives exist for motivating proactive participation by the organization or program being reviewed.

A frequent feeling of those being audited is that the audits often fail to adequately identify root causes and instead spotlight issues only where they manifest themselves, not where they originate. A review of hiring practices for example might uncover a series of continuous layers of issues being uncovered with programs pointing to long hiring cycles driving away the best candidates, followed by the human resources department pointing to regulatory compliance and long candidate review by programs, followed by programs pointing to the inclusion of non-qualified resources in the list of candidates, and so on. In actuality all of these issues may be accurate and correctly identified but that doesn't mean knowing them easily translates into knowing how to solve them. The true root causes may lead back to unintended consequences of well-meaning legislation but how is an organization's management going to easily fix that? While it realistically can't it may certainly be blamed for its impact.

After a number of these reviews or audits, government personnel are frequently left to wonder why no one seems interested in asking what they need to be successful, only whether they are. Simply embedding the question, 'what do you need to be successful?' in most audits and reviews uncovers a wealth of ideas across the government from those that know the problem best; the individuals embedded in, managing, or performing the related activities.

Ultimately, the reliance on and abundance of formal and informal audits and reviews creates over time a culture typically adverse to providing real visibility into operations and performance. This increased defensiveness and reduced visibility represents another of the many realities making change significantly more difficult in the public sector.

Individuals attempting to improve performance or increase efficiency in the public sector are often trying to steer a large ship with a small rudder. The traditional leverage required for large-scale changes simply doesn't exist in most government organizations. By definition, any successful changes will occur in smaller degrees over longer periods of time. The concepts described in Sections 4-12 within this book have proven successful because given these common characteristics, they support incremental change in environments with complex structures and non-traditional motivators.

Trends Driving Change
in the Public Sector

Some consider the need for and frequency of change in the public sector to be lower than in the private sector. After all, the reasoning goes, the private sector is under constant pressure from the market to innovate, adapt, and take advantage of opportunity. The public sector by comparison is considered, even by some that work in it, to be more stable, requiring reduced speed and frequency of change commensurate with the environment. The reality is that the public sector's agenda and activity are often driven by a much larger pool of events which impact the government more frequently and in significantly greater ways than those in the private sector.

9

Transition from Routine to Project-Oriented Activities

Similar to trends seen in many service and information fields, public sector organizations are transitioning away from managing routine duties that stay consistent from day to day and year to year towards activities that are more project-oriented - collections of activities with specific and limited objectives. Unlike routine duties, projects are structured for limited duration activities, possessing a beginning, middle, and end. This larger shift in the way an organization's activities are carried out is causing a major change in the way public sector organizations manage their missions and associated activities.

In a project-oriented world, the traditional investments an organization makes in support infrastructure and automated processes often result in little payoff. Instead, project activities favor technologies that can be quickly implemented and customized to meet temporary needs and shuttered or archived at the conclusion of efforts. For example, projects often require a calendar and scheduling function as well as a website where people can post information and files. To meet these needs, many organizations are turning to technologies such as Microsoft® SharePoint® or similar platforms for rapid collaboration and information sharing. The ability to rapidly deploy a set of capabilities to a new project team instead of deploying large-scale custom systems directly impacts the way public sector IT organizations operate.

A phenomenon seen in many organizations is a lack of awareness of the type and nature of activity they're truly engaged in. In some organizations, permanent functions receive little thought and investment as if the function is temporary like a project. In other cases, significant investment is made in documentation and supporting systems for a specific project which, after completed, has little future value to the organization. This incongruity of investment with activity permanence often inhibits the effectiveness of both ongoing functions as well as projects.

The individual skill sets required in an organization are also changing. Individuals who specialize in 'getting things done' are becoming more valuable over those who know 'how to get something specific done'. The change in skill sets are requiring organizations to change the way they approach human capital management including recruiting and training their personnel. Even the ways organizations are structured are changing because of this shift in activity focus. The nature of projects tends to drive a need for multi-disciplinary involvement, making the traditional functional structure of organizations increasingly less meaningful. Instead the need to rapidly pull individuals across sub-organizations together is driving an increase in the use of matrix-oriented organizational structures.

The increase in project-oriented efforts ultimately affects almost every aspect of public sector organizations -

from technical and human capital resources to the way organizations track budgets, costs, and performance. The success of this transition in activity and focus is contingent in large part on the extent to which required organizational changes are formally contemplated and managed.

10

Multiple Internal and External Agendas

A combination of new scrutiny and focus by the President's administration on various agency activities along with increasing reviews by internal and external watchdogs such as OMB and GAO are forcing organizations to change their existing approaches. The current President, Barack Obama, has appointed a number of individuals to leadership positions with the attitude that the status quo is not acceptable. Indeed, this is the position of virtually all newly elected Presidents which leads to a nearly constant desire for change in the way public sector organizations operate.

The reality though for most government agencies is that the desired changes will take significantly longer than typically envisioned, often extending beyond when the next administration will appoint new leadership with its own and likely different vision. To avoid the tumult, many career government managers look to naturally limit the amount of change a new administration makes in order to maintain some stability and reduce the amount of organizational upheaval as the executive and legislative pendulums swing back and forth.

The 'study' for example often proves a useful tool in creating an immediate response to external direction without immediately dictating or driving actual change. While at face value, the perennial 'study-loop' may appear to be a lack of understanding or motivation to embrace real change; in reality the mechanism is sometimes simply a tool to create drag that allows an organization more time to assess the permanence of the external direction. Once leadership perceives a direction or decision to be universally consistent or appropriate, change activities may be initiated.

In many cases, internal and external agendas may also conflict. For example, the legislative branch may demand accountability for a specific level of spend on an agency program. Congress may ask for justification and put forth a belief that the same objective could be accomplished with less funding. But when the organization attempts to achieve a reduction based on identifying efficiencies such as combining or centralizing positions, letters to Congressmen from affected employees or unions may result in the same legislative officials pushing back on the agency to avoid cuts in their own state or district. The result is the agency simply puts more effort into justifying the current level than seeking efficiencies.

The objectives and focuses of internal and external watchdogs also change along with executive and legislative leadership, but their impact tends to be more targeted to specific programs or functional areas. The results of reviews or audits by these organizations can drive little or significant change, depending on the level with which the scrutinized groups and organizational leadership embrace the results. In reality, most of these groups lack meaningful punitive mechanisms or formal authority to direct immediate and specific changes. When the scrutiny results in higher-profile findings however, the change effect can be immediate and significant for the subject areas reviewed.

11

Shrinking and Expanding Budgets

This administration and Congress, like others, seeks to manage governmental activities and focuses by adjusting the budgets of various government organizations. In some cases, budgets are increased to fund areas of particular focus of an administration or members of Congress. When these funds are substantial, they may drive the need to create new permanent organizations or programs. For example, financial reforms driven by the housing and financial crises of the past few years has resulted in the formation of several new organizations to oversee reform or enforce new industry rules. However, some in Congress are already working to identify ways to eliminate, shrink, or alter the structure and mission of these new organizations.

In some cases, when the funds are both significant and temporary, organizations face the double-whammy of both ramping up to spend the funding and unwinding what was created to manage and spend the increased funds. The President's American Recovery and Reinvestment Act of 2009 (ARRA) is a great example of a spending event that drove great change in public sector organizations; some permanent, some temporary as agencies raced to spend funds on a wide-variety of large-scale projects and services efforts. The act's new reporting requirements alone drove organizations to bring on new staff, invest in new technologies, and create new contract support vehicles - many of which will exist in some form or another for years to come.

Shrinking budgets likewise force change on public sector organizations. To reduce its spending, organizations are forced to shutter specific activities or enforce cross-cutting reductions often of a specific percentage. These activities often drive new initiatives to find opportunities to reduce costs, especially in support functions in order to preserve as much as possible the mission-oriented activities of the organization. The need to shut down programs or reduce costs itself often drives the creation of new contemplative bodies designed to assess which programs or activities should stay and which are cut.

The up and down funding cycles of many government programs and organizations is a good example of the intractable issues government managers face. Efforts to change the model may prove futile, but responding to and addressing the changes created by them remain a necessity.

12

Increasing Market Complexity

Changes in private sector markets, as well as their increasing complexity, often drives changes in the government organizations which monitor and regulate markets. Public sector regulatory and oversight organizations must continuously re-evaluate the manner in which they approach, monitor, and manage their respective markets in order to achieve their oversight missions. From inspection activities to proposed changes in the law, many public sector organizations are impacted by continual market evolution.

The Nuclear Regulatory Commission for example, is addressing the re-emergence of nuclear power as an acceptable clean, safe, and efficient energy alternative. The increase in license applicants is driving the agency to increase hiring, build new facilities, and update its processes and technologies. The Federal Trade Commission (FTC) is re-evaluating its approach to trade regulation and combating anti-competitive practices based on the increasingly global competitive environment fueled by technologies such as the internet. The rapid increase in and adoption of new consumer technologies, accompanied by new types of fraud, have forced the FTC to adapt its identification and response approaches. The Federal Communications Commission is continuously creating, evaluating, and revising rules based on the rapid innovation occurring in telecommunications and information distribution. The impact of increased market complexity and activity levels is forcing these government organizations and others to adjust their focuses, resource levels, and competencies in as rapid a manner as possible to keep pace with industry change.

The greater the market changes, the greater the public sector change required. In some cases the changes result in the creation or consolidation of entire federal organizations. In some cases, more sudden larger-scale changes are easier than less significant ones for public sector organizations to address. Public and legislative pressure along with the increased visibility of the government response drops a lot of natural barriers to change. Smaller-scale changes often prove more difficult for public sector organizations to address. Changes with low profiles are often the most difficult to address until required changes reach a critical mass, elevating their profile and pushing them into a category that garners legislative, executive, or wider-scale attention. Trying to keep pace in the meantime often requires the heavy use of the public sector change management techniques described in this book.

13

External Threats
and Other Events

Change is also thrust upon government organizations through a variety of external events such as the threat and realization of physical disasters, whether natural or terrorism related. As the level of external events becomes more dynamic, public sector organizations are often tasked with adjusting their focuses accordingly. Cyber security for example, which few public sector organizations worried about just a decade ago, now consumes significant public sector resources. The need to address one to two security events a year a decade ago has changed over time, now requiring many public sector organizations to address hundreds of attempts per day by hackers across the globe.

The external threat driver is a great mechanism for illustrating the scale and complexity of missions for public sector organizations. While private sector organizations expend resources identifying and mitigating their individual risks, many public sector organizations are tasked with identifying and mitigating specific types of risks for *all* businesses and industries. This mission, while similar in functional requirement to the private sector, is exponentially larger in terms of the scope of risk and resources required to effectively mitigate it. In some cases the appropriate level of public sector resources are deployed and in other cases resources may be lacking, but in either case the sheer number of moving parts results in a massively evolving landscape of required changes to remain effective at mitigating risk and responding to potential and actual events.

At the macro level, where most political decision-makers operate, the broad strokes of change may be obvious. But imagine the operational environment of trying to respond to evolving threats. New risks equals new competency requirements. But simply hiring and on-boarding new staff might take 4-6 months; and that's after positions are created and requisitions are approved. Training existing staff might also take months as funds are identified and allocated and travel is approved. Compare this to one private sector organization that kept $500,000 in petty cash on the executive floor in their New York offices in case someone needed something quickly - and approval was only an e-mail away.

As the threats to our nation change, so must those organizations tasked with protecting it. New ways to gather and analyze information, develop responses, and mobilize resources all drive change in the way public sector organizations must operate.

By no means exhaustive, there are many factors that drive the need for public sector organizations to change either periodically or continuously, often in ways so significant, there are simply no parallels in the private sector. While adjusting to these factors may be built into the models of many of the government organizations, often times they play out in more subtle ways which put organizations behind the curve in terms of needed change.

Traditional Elements
of Change Management

The art and science of getting things done in any organization has always included a mastery of the traditional elements of change management. Doing things differently to some extent, lies at the heart of virtually all projects and initiatives within government. But getting an organization to do things differently almost always starts with getting its people to do things differently.

Opposing any change is a series of natural barriers, many of which may be erected by an organization's individuals. However, put simply, change is hard, it's uncomfortable, and to a large extent, people in almost all organizations prefer the status quo no matter how painful, over the pain associated with changes to it. To address this, the discipline of change management has evolved over time to encompass a combination of logistical and change-oriented techniques designed to help efforts move forward.

14

Using Project Management Disciplines

Although this is not a book about project management, the core concepts of project management play a significant role in successful change efforts. Identifying goals or the desired end state provide the direction virtually all efforts need. A schedule outlining the activities, their sequencing, and who specifically will complete them acts as the basic roadmap for reaching the desired end state. Finally, shepherding the effort by managing the activities over time and course correcting when necessary moves the effort forward along the path. These basic activities provide the foundation and ongoing framework in which most successful change efforts live.

Like many skills, successful project management is a combination of art and science, blending the core concepts of the discipline with the experience of knowing when and how to best apply those concepts. Although the discipline can be studied and learned, only through experience of actually managing efforts does one master the skill. Like many recent books on talent development have pointed out, as many as 10,000 hours of actual practice may be required to develop mastery. A lack of appreciation for the value of individuals with the right combination of education and experience has caused more than one project to fail in the public sector. In some cases a resource, no matter how much time they're given and how many courses they have taken, just can't manage projects - all core project management skills rest on a foundation of common sense which can't be taught.

The core aspects of project management are often commingled with public sector contract and task order management concepts with the two often viewed interchangeably. Good project management is about getting things done in the most effective manner given a variety of variables and constraints. Good contract and task management is often about managing the 'burn' rate of dollars, adhering to required clauses, and following required compliance steps. Both are valuable and when each is effectively executed, efforts are well on their way to a successful conclusion. However, when one is confused for the other, gaps in either may become significant enough to derail efforts. In reality, contracts and tasks can be successfully administered without actually getting anything done and conversely, projects can be managed to deliver intended benefits but fail to execute a number of other required activities peripheral to the effort's primary work-streams.

An important project management distinction between public and private sector organizations is the emphasis on sequencing over date-driven activity scheduling in the public sector. The de-emphasis on date-driven activities stems from the reality that for many government change efforts, the culture and other intractable obstacles, not logistics and available resource levels, drive the actual schedule. Understanding and managing this reality is one of several concepts that differentiate public from private sector change management.

15

Building the Right Team

An essential step in launching a successful change effort is building a core team of resources to support or participate in an effort. Even if the change is small in scale or scope, the ability to develop formal and informal teams to support an effort represents a critical activity for change efforts. These resources provide the horsepower for accomplishing the required tasks associated with moving the organization forward.

In many cases, a change leader will find themselves assigned a group of individuals to work with, sometimes representing a collection of the most appropriate resources to support an effort. Though in many cases in both the public and private sectors, a team is developed based on a combination of organizational representation and individuals perceived to have free time. The ability to leverage the good while minimizing the distractions often represents the difference between a successful team and an ineffectual one.

For change efforts, identifying and leveraging (or mitigating) individual personalities often proves as important as identifying and leveraging individual skills and interests. As mentioned earlier, the variety of organizational personalities, which includes individuals with little motivation to actively participate as well as those with opposite agendas, can significantly alter the pace and direction of change.

The most effective teams are typically constructed by first identifying an individual to lead the effort followed by that leader working with organizational leadership to recruit 'hand-picked' resources. Often times however, various organizations are asked to volunteer individuals to participate, in which case the team composition is left largely to chance. Additional techniques identified in later chapters are designed specifically to help keep efforts moving even when change leaders are dealt heavy doses of less than ideal participants.

Another major factor in building teams to support efforts is the reality that virtually all assigned individuals, potentially even an effort's leaders, are part time resources with 'day' jobs. Without a true vested interest, many resources, especially volunteered resources, view participation as simply something they must do - which often results in a natural desire to do the minimum necessary to get by. Effective change leaders employ a variety of push and pull techniques to try and motivate the team to engage and stay engaged productively in the effort. Leaders that recognize that the team's resources have other demands and work to limit and balance team activities for individuals tend to generate better trust and dedication over the course of an effort.

16

Creating or Finding
Self Interest

Another common technique used to move efforts forward is finding and attempting to satisfy the 'what's in it for me' question within a given change effort. In some cases this is a great motivator; the ability to show individuals impacted by change the direct benefits to them personally often facilitates progress. However, this technique, which commonly represents the key recommended lever for many change efforts, is often over or misused. In cases where the benefits aren't for those who need to change but instead realized by those they serve in some capacity, the 'what's in it for me approach' rings appropriately disingenuous. 'You mean it's going to be better for me to learn this whole new thing so life is easier for someone else?' When applied where its applicability is tenuous at best, the self-interest lever risks the credibility of the effort as a whole. When appropriate however, the technique often creates leverage for moving efforts forward.

Because self-interest driven by direct benefit is often inapplicable, the more common self-interest lever used in the public sector is self-preservation. Fear of personal failure, organizational breakdowns, system failures, or high-profile issues simply drive change better than, 'hey, this is going to save us time and money.' Self-preservation as a lever occurs at almost every level of government. From congressional legislation to implementing a new financial control, the reality is many such actions are taken or changes implemented only when anxiety or fear levels reach a tipping point.

The leadership of the US Postal Service, as an example, know this. Although they have already identified in study after study the need to take action to remain solvent, the needed legislation and authorization for change probably will not come until the last minute - when the reality of the situation translates into immediate fear of collapse. As identified in a later chapter, understanding this reality can prove to be a useful tool in effective public sector change management.

17

Using Power to
Dictate Change

Another traditional change technique is simply using a decree from leadership to dictate change across an organization. This technique, used in conjunction with others is usually appropriate in private sector organizations for many types of changes. Change 'because we pay you to do what we ask' is the essence of the understanding between private sector leadership and employee. Consolidation of several call centers? Pick the one to survive, offer relocation packages to the best resources, and work with HR to prepare severance for the rest. Change complete.

But in public sector organizations, this type of change technique is far less common. Leaders in public sector organizations rarely manage by decree as a rule. Their political capital and goodwill both up and down the organization, along with maintaining good working relationships with a variety of stakeholders, from unions to external constituents, drives a typically softer approach. That same consolidation of call centers? The public sector manager is going to have to get (and keep) every layer of the organization on board and brace for probable backlash from any number of sources. Calls from Congressmen for example, asking the public sector manager's boss's boss to explain why his office is getting calls about job cuts in their district.

Another issue with simply dictating change in the public sector is that the primary obstacles to change in government typically have little to do with 'what' needs to happen. The biggest issues lie in 'how' things happen. Even Congress and other law and rule-making entities typically dictate only what organizations need to do, rarely venturing into how to get it done. Although it may seem appropriate, the high-level edict for a result leaves each organization free to develop its own implementation path, resulting in potentially dozens of unique and singular paths to the same end across the government landscape.

18

Training New Skills
and Behaviors

Many traditional change efforts rely heavily on the concept of re-training to drive change, looking to 're-engineer' the individual to look at issues or perform tasks differently. For the most part, teaching individuals new skills or re-training them to perform activities differently does drive acceptance and help facilitate change.

However, virtually all training organizations provide to employees related to implemented changes focuses on new or revised functional skills - how to use a new system or use different procedures. An often overlooked area of training is teaching managers how to manage their parts of the organization *through* the change. Skills and ideas on how to problem solve, drive acceptance, or facilitate group discussions when appropriately timed go a long way towards moving an organization along a path. The skills themselves are useful but perhaps equally important is the feeling of inclusion the targeted training provides managers. The focus and investment on the role of the manager as a change agent actually drives managers to feel more responsible for the change succeeding. Managers feel like they're part of and have some control over the change, as opposed to something that is simply also happening to them.

The best training programs that accompany change efforts contemplate and incorporate all of the required skills - starting with new functional or technical skills but also include communications training for liaisons or individuals charged with outreach, change management for managers, and training for support resources such as IT, HR, and finance for example. Ideally, training is timed so that there is little lag between the training and when the newly acquired skills and information can be exercised. Training tends to have a very short half-life and after a couple weeks, if the training is not put to use, 90% or more of the material is forgotten. The very best programs also phase in the material over several sessions or a period of time so the right skills are taught for the right phases as needed. This approach supports not only the timing but provides repetition to improve retention.

The use of training alone typically does not fully institutionalize desired changes within an organization. However, as a companion to other change activities, training represents a key public and private sector lever when used correctly.

19

Charting the
People Landscape

Identifying and managing the key players associated with or impacted by a change is another common element of traditional change management efforts. Identifying these individuals or groups in the private sector is considered necessary for an efficient transition. In the public sector, the necessity to identify the various seats of formal and informal power and their relative positions and interests adds an additional emphasis to this activity.

Charting and managing the people landscape often starts with identifying who support is needed from and deciding how to obtain that support. In some cases these individuals are already natural supporters while in other cases they may be on the fence or even net detractors from an effort. In the public sector for example, the consolidation of one organization into another will likely consist of individuals and groups backing the effort, typically the leadership of the larger organization; and those opposed, typically the individuals who will lose power, authority, and autonomy. Determining the best approach for each individual and the order of battle is often important to the success of the effort over time.

Often the result of an examination of the people landscape will conclude that there is no way to get all of the opposed 'on board'. Instead, the effort focuses on getting those who will gain to use their resources and influence to push the effort forward. To address those opposed, the approach sometimes includes either winning enough detractors over by giving a small handful of influential detractors key roles (buying their support) or determining the best way to neutralize their opposition.

Another important component of planning from a human capital perspective is identifying the targets of change and developing a plan for approaching and managing these individuals to maximize the probability of a successful effort. In private sector organizations, this is frequently accomplished by a combination of frequent communication and appropriately timed training. In public sector organizations, the targets are often in the driver's seat and their cooperation and collaboration is critical. Without their buy-in, the targets will often simply 'wait-out' the change agent until they move on. In one organization, impacted staff exercised almost every lever at their disposal to scuttle a re-organization. Their efforts included contacting Congressmen, activating union representatives to write the agency's leadership, failing to provide key information to planners, and perhaps most importantly, out maneuvering the effort's planners in identifying organizational leaders still on the fence and lobbying those individuals to delay the effort.

A few years ago, another agency sought to close some of

its infrequently used physical libraries and replace them with a virtual library given that most of the materials and periodicals were available electronically. Although the effort would have saved millions, a handful of individuals lobbied outside organizations to petition the agency to keep the libraries open. The outside organization used a number of media outlets to paint the initiative as cutting critical mission support instead of fat. Given the press, the agency backed off its plans to close the libraries. However, since the agency had already started the effort and procured electronic materials and subscriptions, the result was an even higher cost structure for the delivery of library services.

What these examples illustrate is that the best efforts invest the time to identify and message to various stakeholders because someone will - and if it isn't the effort's leaders, it will almost certainly be its opponents.

20

Selling the Future

Selling is often a major component of change efforts. Selling the benefits, selling the future, selling the vision of the shining city on the hill which an organization must march towards is commonly used to motivate the masses. While the effectiveness of selling change in the public sector is often diminished in organizations with repeated failures to reach the 'city', selling is still an important technique successful change leaders commonly leverage.

The ability to paint the picture of success, with all its benefits, is an important lever. However, balancing that sales effort with the practicalities of the environment and what is reasonably achievable has proven equally important. Over-selling often creates different kinds of risks and failure to deliver the expected benefits has typically resulted in individual reputational damage and adds to a typically already jaundiced culture in public sector organizations.

Anxious to get a new approach to managing travel implemented, one agency manager painted a very compelling vision in PowerPoint, describing the organizational benefits and emphasizing the ease with which travel could be arranged, adhere to federal requirements, and provide top down visibility for leadership into travel spending. Inevitably the manager was unable to deliver the full benefits of the system and the effort was described by many as a failure, even though some benefits were realized and additional benefits would be realized over time.

Another potential limitation of change efforts that rely heavily on selling the future is that they tend to minimize the impact of *transitioning* to the future. Often times the future is ideal, but the rub for an organization and its individuals is the pain and friction of getting there. An end-state vision is often translated sub-consciously into magical transportation to a new operating model or business paradigm. The pain of change, real and psychological is typically left off the vision 'sales brochure'. Once people start feeling the pain of change (where's my position in this org chart!?) the vision often goes out the window.

One agency manager, for example, wanted to consolidate economists into one organization instead of having individuals reporting into a separate organization in a decentralized fashion. The stated vision described a better career path for individuals, giving them more options as economists within an economics group as opposed to a singular role in one organization. The majority of individuals were on board but once the impact of geographies, pay grades, defining roles, who would report to whom, what the processes would look like for organizations to leverage the group, and other transition realities shook out, many who once favored the change became resistant to the effort.

Selling the future also involves, to a large extent, the creation of a holistic vision, which often translates into a 'big' change. This would seem to make sense; given that that a vision built on 'we're going to evolve incrementally, potentially crawling at times, slowly into a better model,' doesn't have the same appeal. But 'big' visions can scare people, from leaders to staff, pushing them into a fear zone that change tends to invoke. For example, one federal organization tried to promote the use of a new technology to manage data. The vision was beautifully articulated, describing a new paradigm with enormous benefit to industry, taxpayers, and other stakeholders. The idea sat for years as leader after leader rejected it as too costly and risky. Only after the approach was changed to incrementally build and pilot the system did it finally begin to move forward as a real initiative.

Selling the future involves risk. In the private sector, many individuals gladly accept this risk given the personal and professional rewards that await when the effort is successful. In the public sector, with a limited reward structure and high levels of change resistance, many successful change leaders instead develop but 'back-pocket' visions, using them more as personal roadmaps or selectively sharing them when needed.

Traditional change management techniques are not without merit in the public sector. Their appropriate use is important and provides substantially the same benefits as in the private sector. However, given the unique culture, structures, and challenges in government organizations, these techniques must be augmented with a number of other techniques described in the remaining sections. Together the traditional and public sector change management techniques arm an individual with the tools necessary to achieve lasting change in the public sector.

Managing the Pace of Change

In the classic Greek myth, Icarus, attempting to successfully fly across the ocean with wings constructed of wax and feathers must avoid flying too close to the sun or risk the wax melting and avoid flying too close to the sea or risk the feathers getting wet. In the public sector, the need to manage the pace of change is akin to Icarus', managing to a 'right' speed that is neither too fast nor too slow for the organization, always being mindful of the 'sun' and the 'sea'.

21

Faster Does Not
Always Equal Better

Ideally, the pace of any change would be limited only by logistics. In the private sector, opportunities are often taken advantage of as fast as the organization can acquire the right skills and execute. But in the public sector individuals need to balance the rate of change with the organization's ability to keep pace. If change exceeds the natural rate of the organization, its individuals will lack the ability to 'consume' the changes, resulting in increased apprehension and eventually revolt.

The introduction of new concepts and potential changes are ideally paced at a speed where individuals are allowed time to adjust, but no slower than is necessary for this to occur. Adapting too slowly creates different kinds of risks, both organizationally as well as professionally, ranging from an inability to meet or comply with certain requirements or being seen as personally ineffectual. As one federal organization attempted to implement a shared services model for human resources for example, the effort's sponsor specifically held meetings no more often than monthly at the beginning. Although logistically the whole effort could have been completed in sixty days, the sponsor expressed the belief that the only way to ensure agreement and buy-in was to pace the transition so that it purposely took at least six months. He stated that in his almost thirty years in the organization, he noticed that people typically fought change for the first several months no matter how often they met, but after the third month they started getting used to the idea and generally came around. His belief was that people needed time to both think about something as well as accept that it wasn't going to go away.

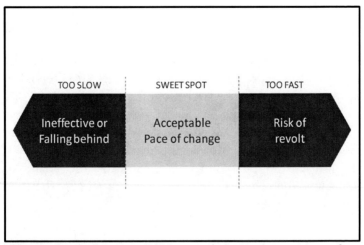

Figure 5: Finding the right pace of change between too fast and too slow is critical to successful change efforts.

There is no explicit formula that dictates the right pace for a given organization or effort. Individuals simply need to be aware of the pace of their efforts to ensure they are moving as fast as they can, but no faster than the organization can handle.

A common sign an effort is exceeding the ideal pace is when growing numbers of individuals both inside and outside the effort increasingly lose track of what's going on or begin to question the effort's objectives and value. The inability to 'follow the plot' as efforts pick up pace can breed apprehension which triggers the risk averse nature of the organization, resulting in a natural desire by the organization and its employees to slow the effort down.

Although the consequences of progressing too slowly are rarer, a common sign an effort is moving too slow is when increasing numbers of individuals begin to question project progress or productivity. If this is occurring, the change leader must evaluate what practical techniques are available to accelerate the pace.

Since many individuals simply don't contemplate the issues associated with going too fast, they naturally support a faster pace until the organizational 'noise level' rises. Being mindful of the organizational noise and the effort's pace is an important lever for successful incremental change.

22

The Awareness Tipping Point

Another important pace of change concept is the 'awareness tipping point'. The awareness tipping point is the point at which an otherwise unknown or unobtrusive effort captures the attention of the masses. Controlling the tipping point represents a significant factor in the ability to accomplish real change.

The ideal strategy for many change efforts is to build as much momentum and buy-in as possible before crossing the threshold of critical mass awareness. By limiting communication to selected individuals and moving forward with as much lower-profile planning activities as possible, an effort can build energy and support with reduced organizational resistance. With the groundwork laid and enough momentum, efforts have a better chance of making it through the natural organizational inhibitors of progress.

By delaying the tipping point, an effort's plans are more complete, the right allies have been brought in, risks are better identified, and the time available for others to develop counter-strategies has been minimized. Without more time to develop reasons not to do something, many obstacles that might have otherwise appeared are bypassed.

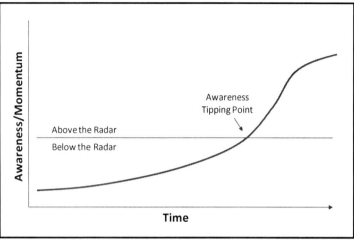

Figure 6: Staying 'below the radar' longer helps efforts build momentum without triggering material levels of resistance.

Although many efforts have natural 'quick wins', individuals must fully assess their desirability relative to 'tipping one's hand' too early. Quick wins do help establish momentum and gain broader buy-in, but their early visibility is sometimes a negative to the accomplishment of longer term change efforts. In addition, any early visible issues encountered will likely be used as ammunition by detractors against more substantive efforts. This is not to imply quick wins should never be taken advantage of. However individuals need to think through them like a chess player thinks about future moves. An early strike may ultimately reveal a strategy too soon and leave key pieces vulnerable and out of place.

23

Avoiding Over-Communication

Effective communications are often pointed to as a critical element of any change strategy. The prevailing opinion is often that there is no such thing as too much communication. Keeping everyone fully informed is often the communications goal of an effort. This belief however can introduce additional and unnecessary risks to change efforts.

In addition to potentially tipping awareness, communications commonly increase expectations. Moreover, individuals are often advised or instructed by leadership to 'sell the benefits' to achieve interest and buy-in. But once these expectations are set, an inability to meet them only further adds to an already skeptical culture and can hurt personal credibility. One organization spent months touting the new features of a soon to go-live financial system. Unfortunately the new system's interface proved difficult to use and some features were dropped in the initial version to get it in production on time. Users were not kind in their feedback of the new system - almost every user who provided feedback sited the promises made.

Communications associated with how long something will take possesses the same risk. Hard dates are rarely met and their broad communication early on drives almost no value. As dates move closer, along with the increased likelihood of the accuracy, communication of them makes more sense. In one organization for example, a large poster was put up in 2005 that spanned an entire hallway showing the two year implementation for a reorganization. In 2010, though the reorganization was still in progress, the poster was removed after someone asked the organization's deputy administrator when the hallway would get 'new wallpaper'.

Over a period of time and a series of projects and activities, missed promises and dates reduce or destroy an organization's credibility. Unless early communications are absolutely necessary, a better approach is often to just deliver results, and then communicate the heck out of the success and its benefits. This approach lowers risk and increases an individual's personal brand as someone who can consistently execute and deliver.

Monica recently joined a civilian agency as an Associate Director of Finance in its Office of the Chief Financial Officer (CFO). One of the first goals the CFO wanted Monica to accomplish was to establish mechanisms for getting each program to use a standard method and format for formulating its budgets. The CFO believed the current method for many sub-organizations in this agency was to simply incrementally increase last year's budget for each of its major programs but he desired increased discipline in the process.

The CFO's office had historically established a good history of working collaboratively with the program offices but the current CFO was not well liked based on a number of unilateral policy changes such as increasing the frequency of reporting. Even less material changes such as restricting the use of the CFO title in the organization had further weakened the CFO's political capital within the program offices.

Faster does not Always Equal Better
Monica learned from a series of informal discussions with program office personnel that the concept of 'bottom up' or activity-based budgeting had been tried several times over the last couple decades but those efforts failed either by dying under their own weight or people simply waiting out the politically appointed leaders driving the demand for it. The CFO asked Monica to simply create and issue new

policies dictating the change in approach but Monica pushed back given that this approach had failed in the past. Monica understood that for this effort to be successful she needed to pace this effort so that the organization had time to adopt and adapt, but she also needed to manage upwards as well to help the CFO understand that this simply wasn't going to happen overnight.

The Awareness Tipping Point

To start positioning the organization for a transition, Monica assembled a core group of program office stakeholders who, through her discussions, she had identified as allies in implementing a new budgeting process and developed a ninety day plan for the development and testing of the modified approach. Monica described the effort as a proof of concept and asked the stakeholders to downplay the effort to the organization in order to minimize confusion.

Avoid Over-communication

Monica's contractor support urged her to broadcast the effort to start building support by conveying the expected benefits to the organization. From previous experience Monica recognized that these efforts almost always create more work for program offices with minimal immediate benefit.

Unless the tools were in place to help the offices collect the data they needed, analyze it, and capture their budget decisions based on it, this effort would likely fail like those before it. Monica instead focused on building, testing, and refining the capabilities needed before marketing them.

Conclusion - Using PS Change Techniques

After developing a set of tools to facilitate the process, Monica asked several offices to pilot the approach by using it on one program area each for the next fiscal year programming effort. While some groups protested a bit initially, the tools and method Monica crafted allowed room for minimal defense and each office complied. Monica collected feedback from each office, sought to expand her group of allies in the cause, and further refined the tools and approach for an expanded pilot the following year.

Conclusion - Not Using PS Change Techniques

Monica complied with the CFO's desire to issue a policy dictating the change in approach. The issuance of the policy represented an organization-wide broadcast which resulted in several offices immediately offering counter-arguments and positions on budget processes. Some offices announced that they too were looking into improved approaches and would not comply until their own reviews were completed. The unilateral policy approach reduced what little political capital Monica had and a series of communications expounding on the virtues of the CFO approach only further painted Monica as naive in the eyes of the program offices. Ultimately, with so much resistance, the CFO agreed to delay implementation of the policy and Monica was viewed as ineffectual by both the program offices and the CFO.

Managing the pace of change, controlling the awareness tipping point, and avoiding over-communication represent foundational levers for making progress in public sector organizations. Without the awareness of these concepts, individuals run the risk of 'winning battles but losing the war' when traditional techniques enable some progress but ultimately stall the larger effort.

Segmenting Change

Big change in any organization is hard. The reasons for this are covered by decades of research and documented in hundreds of books and studies. Much of this research is summarized by a common saying that people simply prefer the 'certainty of misery' to the 'misery of uncertainty', and this often holds true in public and private sector organizations alike. However, without the private sector levers of more decisive leadership, command and control structures, and the ability to fully leverage techniques that make change stick, public sector organizations face significantly unique and greater challenges changing things.

24

Segmenting Efforts

One of the keys to successfully executing large-scale change in public sector organizations is breaking down the effort into much smaller changes or efforts, the combination of which ultimately implements a larger scale change. Smaller changes help reduce complexity for the implementer as well as the organization, they're easier for people to adjust to, and their value is more easily justified.

Segmenting change is different from segmenting activity or breaking a plan into sub-tasks. Segmenting change focuses on identifying the right level of achievable progress towards a goal and moving forward with that change. Efforts may possess a combination of larger and smaller segments but each is based on identifying what is necessary and only necessary to feasibly move forward. For example, if an organization wanted to improve the efficiency of its fleet operations, the initial thought might be to simply identify ways to reduce costs by looking at the organization's fleet requirements, analyzing some operational scenarios or performing a present value analysis on investments and then executing. However, the reality might be that the fleet itself is managed by seven regional centers all doing their own thing. Improvement will likely require standardization or even centralized management. The only truly feasible approach is to heavily segment the effort. Those segments themselves may need to be segmented again and again perhaps starting simply with an initial goal of getting the regional fleet managers together for the first time.

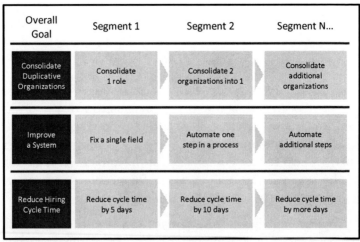

Figure 7: Examples of segmenting different types of change into smaller, more manageable efforts.

In organizations highly resistant to change or ones in which significant cultural or political resistance exists, it may be necessary to continue to segment efforts into what might almost be described as micro-changes. The result is, as one might imagine, micro-progress at first, but as progress is made over time through a series of small changes, the effort starts to reach a point of critical mass, a point at which the change is unstoppable based on momentum.

25

Focusing on Direction
Over Destination

When an initiative is broken into segments, the direction of those segments becomes more critical, often more important than the destination itself. A key benefit of segmentation is that even though a broad, large-scale objective may never be fully achieved, the successful execution of one or more smaller efforts typically results in real incremental value for the organization. From this perspective, success is measured not by the implementation of a 'thing' but by progress achieved towards a set of objectives.

Take for example the concept of consolidation. Whether the focus is redundant organizations, roles, or systems, if the goal is to consolidate it down to one, every stakeholder must buy in completely to achieve that goal. However, if the effort is segmented into smaller efforts where receptive groups consolidate first, followed by the consolidation of a few more groups that were straddling the fence, even if the remaining groups refuse to budge redundancy is significantly reduced. Progress is made regardless of whether the ultimate goal is ever achieved. This shift in approach, though frequently subtle, can suddenly generate progress where previously none seemed possible.

Embracing this concept often solves another point of paralysis for efforts, taking the first step. Many efforts are stalled at the point of transition from vision or plan to action because that initial step represents a complete and total buy-in to the whole concept or destination. By removing that burden from the first point of action, and instead framing that the first step may also be the last if it makes sense, the ability to move forward is often enabled. When one federal organization was considering whether to support a public-private initiative to build a new type of plant, the effort went through years of internal debate. Once a decision was made to just kick-off formal planning with industry because that alone would offer enormous value even if they didn't move forward after that, progress on design, information sharing, and innovation was enabled.

26

Minimizing the Scope
and Scale of Decisions

Decisions, to a large extent, create natural risk for the individuals making them. A common strategy for many leaders is to minimize this risk and the need to personally extend themselves through explicit decision-making. Instead, these leaders seek to 'engineer' outcomes through a variety of mechanisms. In some cases, the engineered outcome is equivalent to an explicit decision by the leader. But in many cases, the ability to secure explicit decisions from formal leadership is an eventual requirement for true progress.

The reality in many public sector organizations is that decisions can reach a certain level of importance or impact that they simply won't be made by their leadership for professional, political, and personal reasons. Every decision, in the private and public sector, professionally and personally, requires the acceptance of a certain level of risk and often the cashing in of some level of goodwill. The larger the decision, the more risk and the more expense of goodwill and political capital.

The ability to successfully secure formal decisions from public sector leaders is frequently a result of minimizing the scope, scale, and ultimately the risk of those decisions. Decision scope and scale is most easily reduced by creating more frequent decision points focused on smaller scale issues or options consistent with the overall objective. Smaller scale decision points are also a natural result and benefit of efforts that are successfully segmented. An organizational leader for example may refuse to sign-off on a complete re-organization but over time sign-off on the same re-organization in a series of multiple smaller segments.

The number of options presented also represents an important factor in securing formal decisions. More options often result in decision 'paralysis' whereby leadership or other governance mechanisms such as committees are simply overwhelmed by the information they need to process and comprehend in order to make a sound choice. In most cases, the ideal approach is to fully vet options before presentation to leadership for decision making. Ideally the number of options for leadership to consider is limited to two or three. By vetting options thoroughly and reducing their number, the risk of decision 'paralysis' is reduced.

27

Measuring Progress Over Longer Periods of Time

Given the realities of typical public sector environments and cultures, most efforts will simply take longer to complete. Even straightforward activities, such as the release and distribution of a short report can take weeks to complete as the report makes its way through various review cycles. When highly segmented efforts meet the environmental factors of the public sector, progress may be almost unnoticeable except over longer periods of time. Like watching trees grow, looking daily, weekly or even monthly may create the impression that nothing is happening. But from season to season, the progress is unmistakable.

In environments like this with efforts structured in smaller segments, success must be measured over longer periods of time. The adoption of smartphones illustrates this concept. In the private sector, the adoption in organizations was almost immediate. In the public sector however, the use of mobile e-mail and other smartphone functions grew more slowly as security and other requirements were addressed over a period of years. Newer resources entering the public sector workforce, bringing with them a different mindset and demand for the technology, also acted as a catalyst to accelerate organizational adoption. Although this particular transition occurred as a result of more natural forces, the same progress curve exists for concerted efforts to change.

Setting timing expectations accordingly is crucial for maintaining momentum and continued support. Many efforts are launched by the promise of the benefits they will bring. But over promising both the scale and speed with which benefits will come typically leads to discontent and disillusionment, ultimately scuttling otherwise valuable efforts. Balancing value with realistic expectations of extended delivery timing is a key element for successfully moving efforts forward in the public sector.

Bruce was recently promoted to Section Chief within the IT services division of an independent federal agency. His promotion was due in large part to his impressive management over the delivery of IT services to a particular lab within this agency which was a frequent complainer of IT service quality. Bruce knew that a large part of his success stemmed from his ability to establish service level agreements (SLAs) whereby contractor performance was tied specifically to explicit service levels being met for the lab's users. The change had not been easy but the contract was not large and the contractor was amenable to defining specific performance parameters.

Bruce felt that in order to be successful in his new role, he would have to get the agency's largest IT services providers, as well his colleagues and management, to agree to a new performance management model supported by formal SLAs. The concept, while understood by leadership, was a departure from their current qualitative approach. In addition, the organization's IT services were provided by multiple vendors with different contracts for each of its twenty labs and research centers. Bruce felt it would be an uphill climb getting everyone to agree to new contract terms given the various points in the contract lifecycle each contract was currently in, not to mention getting the vendors to agree to what amounted to a more formal evaluation of their performance when they enjoyed the benefits of the current less formal structure.

Segment Efforts

In order to get the effort off the ground, Bruce laid out an initial strategy whereby he would break the effort into five primary phases. First, Bruce would identify the primary metrics valuable for establishing SLAs. Second, Bruce would develop the mechanisms for collecting the metrics, including capturing data from multiple service management applications in use and implementing a simple service quality survey to be completed by the user at the end of any service request. Third, Bruce would work to embed the concept of SLAs into upcoming service contract RFPs. Fourth, Bruce would attempt to negotiate with longer term contract holders the implementation of SLAs into the contract through new and revised task orders under existing vehicles. Lastly, Bruce would look to launch a new effort to consolidate the multiple service management applications as a follow-on project.

Focus on Direction, not Destination

Bruce recognized that he might not be able to fully implement SLAs in every contract, but felt that even getting the organization to think about service levels would drive an increased focus on service quality. Moving beyond that to the collection of data would also provide at a minimum a great snapshot for identifying immediate issues. If Bruce's effort proved more successful, he felt he would be able to get formal SLAs into some if not most of the new and existing contracts.

Minimize the Scope and Scale of Decisions

Bruce was certain that if he tried to consolidate systems and implement an organization-wide standard SLA he would have significant difficulty getting leadership to buy off wholesale on the concept. For one thing, the concept not only spanned multiple sub-organizations in the IT shop but crossed into other functional areas including the acquisition department. He knew from his experience the groups often point fingers when it came to any level of contractual friction. By breaking the effort up, Bruce needed only a handful of individuals to informally discuss what metrics held value, one manager's approval to collect data, and after that, negotiate with individual contract specialists and IT sponsors to start to use them in new or revised contracts.

Measure Progress over Longer Periods of Time

Bruce knew that given the realities of government contracting, the real payoff might take years. Acknowledging this, Bruce explained to his leadership that because the current approach and situation had evolved to its current state over close to two decades, there was simply no easy fix; the solution would take years to fully untangle. Although Bruce expected management to push back, they instead praised him for being honest and being the first to establish not only a vision but a realistic plan.

Conclusion - Using PS Change Techniques

Bruce found that while identifying the metrics was not hard, getting the real data was. Most of the service management systems were run by the contractors themselves and they immediately recognized that making the data readily available was not in their best interests. Bruce escalated his requests and in the end, the contractor resistance to increased visibility would later provide Bruce with additional ammunition for why the service levels were important for improved vendor management. Through the effort, Bruce was eventually able to get SLAs embedded in some tasks within the organization's two largest contracts.

The standardization of the SLAs also enabled the organization to consolidate several other service contracts under one umbrella contract which resulted in other benefits to the organization. The consolidation of service management systems, while valuable, was never implemented because the number of other systems integrated into each system created too much cost and complexity for the effort to be successful. Instead Bruce turned towards other standardization efforts that offered more immediate value to the organization.

Conclusion - Not Using PS Change Techniques

Bruce knew the SLAs represented the lynchpin of improved service. He developed a plan to develop organization wide SLAs, implement a single service management system, and embed the SLAs into every contract. Even after six months of lobbying, Bruce could not get anyone in the organization to sponsor the effort. While the value was clearly greater than the investment, the risk and costs seemed to create an impossible hurdle for getting anyone in leadership to sign up for it. After a year, Bruce finally abandoned the effort leaving many in the organization to conclude that his success at the lab had more to do with being in the right place at the right time than being effective.

Successfully accomplishing change in the public sector frequently requires slicing efforts into as small a chunk of activity as necessary to eliminate resistance. Sometimes changing an organization or program comes down to an ability to make one very small change a day, week, or month - a single field on a form deleted, a single step added to a process, or getting just one person on-board. This 'boil the frog' approach means efforts may take longer, but in some cases the only path forward is a highly incremental one.

Focusing on Benefits and Value

If you pick up almost any book on the subject of project management the primary measures of success are typically defined as the effort being on schedule, on budget, and to specification. Referred to as the 'triple constraints' for the inherent trade-offs between them, these factors are considered critically important in determining an effort's overall success.

However, the reality is there are no shortages of projects across the public sector which meet or exceed all of these measures of success yet are universally considered failures. Many projects fully deliver what was intended on time and budget, however what was created or implemented adds no actual value to the organization. The real success measure - did the organization realize actual value from the project - is rarely considered or measured.

In many cases, duplicative projects or initiatives are launched repeatedly in an attempt to achieve the value of an earlier project when all that was really needed were modest adjustments to the previous effort's implementation. Perhaps minor changes to a process or the configuration of a new organization was all that was needed in order to realize the value the original effort was seeking to deliver.

Take for example many of the requirements OMB places on federal organizations. Tens of millions are spent annually to successfully address the requirements of just one or a few OMB circulars, but the actual value delivered by much of that effort is considered low by many parties.

28

Embedding Benefits Realization into the Life of a Project

Realizing actual benefits from an effort stems heavily from baking activities designed to measure those benefits directly into the plan. In order to realize actual benefits, they need to be identified at the beginning preferably not in the form of high level objectives such as 'increased efficiency or effectiveness' or a working group charter, but the actual benefit expected. By defining the explicit benefits or goals, such as a 'ten day reduction in cycle time', or '30% reduction in complaints', the foundation for measuring progress against an actual benefit is established.

In many public sector organizations, establishing such high levels of specificity regarding expected benefits is considered an unnecessary risk. High level goals with plenty of 'wiggle room' are more compatible with a risk averse culture. In such cases where significant resistance exists to specific goals, using an incrementally increasing approach is often a more viable option. For example, a reduction in cycle time might start with a one day reduction followed by a target of three days, and so on.

As efforts move forward benefits progress should be measured in addition to traditional project metrics such as cost and schedule - specifically evaluating whether activities are in line with realizing the intended benefits. Even status reports should include an analysis of alignment with intended benefits in addition to other items such as completed activities and identified risks.

29

The Value of Post-Implementation Benefits Analysis

One of the best ways to ensure benefits are realized from an effort is to embed the post implementation adjustment activities into the effort itself. By acknowledging the need for and scheduling post-implementation analysis of an effort, the formal opportunity to adjust for improved benefit is created.

What often happens after the implementation of a change is that organizational performance or effectiveness goes down after the rollout. This is a quite common reality but rarely anticipated. What naturally occurs is a decrease in productivity for example based on the need for individuals and the organization to adjust. Unfortunately, this is often mistaken as the result of a failed effort. In some cases, the changes are undone in order to restore the environment to a 'better' operating state. The reality is this effect simply needs to be better anticipated, communicated, and baked into the plan itself.

It's also highly unlikely the initial implementation or changes are perfect, yet so many efforts and plans simply assume that they will be, and thus conclude with the roll-out and logistical transition activities. To increase the actual benefits, the best projects or efforts go beyond 'go live' or traditional completion steps and include post-implementation analysis and refinement. This often missing step is where, in many cases, virtually all of the value of an effort will stem from.

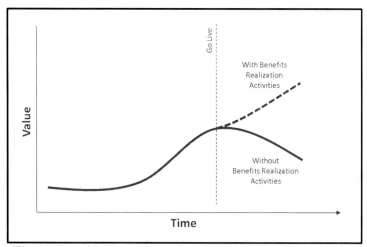

Figure 8: Without a planned and concerted effort to drive benefits after implementation, many efforts fail to realize or sustain value.

By embedding the additional steps of collecting and analyzing performance information and making adjustments, otherwise fruitless efforts are often transformed into successful ones.

30

Using Maturity Models to Measure Performance and Progress

Traditional approaches for measuring performance focus on a classic model of identifying and collecting metrics and reporting them through summary reports or dashboards to management. Improvements are then measured as changes in these metrics. While this approach is better than failing to identify any performance measures, it typically falls significantly short in terms of measuring progress. In some cases, little thought and refinement went into which metrics are meaningful as well as what to do with the information collected. Dashboards may look cool, but often fail to convey meaningful insight.

A gauge by itself for example means nothing. Even real gauges in a factory are designed to start whistling or sound an alarm when a certain level is exceeded. But few corporate dashboards build such business rule equivalents into reporting mechanisms. Ultimately, most dashboards force their users to manage by looking at everything instead of managing by exception. In addition, dashboards and other performance management mechanisms often drive the wrong behavior. Employees, fearful of the repercussions of 'yellows' or 'reds' on a scorecard, are incented to mask issues from management until something more serious reveals the issues after it's sometimes too late to do anything material to mitigate it.

The collection of quantitative metrics is also expensive. The labor to collect or even automate collection can be enormous. For this reason, many successful efforts use the often better and less expensive approach of using a maturity model for assessing the performance of change initiatives. By quickly and somewhat subjectively identifying first what the existing capability is against a basic maturity model, an individual can then define what the organization or effort needs to accomplish to move it to the next level.

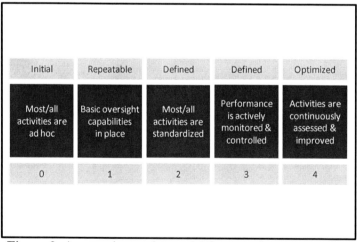

Figure 9: A general maturity model for assessing progress in a more qualitative manner.

An additional benefit of the maturity model approach is that it is a significantly easier story to tell and understand. Occasionally, the desire for a more quantitative approach is driven by a desire by others to see the 'proof', the evidence that change is needed or that something works better. The reality is the collection of real quantitative metrics can be a rabbit hole from which otherwise valuable efforts are never able to climb out. For example, in many cases the real data is held by contractors who have neither the incentive nor the obligation to provide the data needed. With a maturity model approach, the case is often easier – 'we have no automated processes, this entire function is managed on an ad hoc basis so let's just develop and use a basic, repeatable process and our ability to do that *is* the measure of progress.'

In an organization or function with a very low level of overall maturity, anecdotal assessments of performance based on broad strokes are acceptable. Once maturity reaches level three or four, the collection of quantitative metrics may then make sense to drive further incremental value.

Kamal, a project manager in the inspection division of a regulatory agency was asked by his management to join a working group created to look at ways to improve industry inspection processes at his agency. During the first working group meeting, which included equal parts discussing the group's charter and when the group would meet next, Kamal was appointed the group's chair based on his knowledge and tenure. Kamal was excited about the opportunity and saw it as a mechanism for finally addressing the organization's outdated procedures that included references to systems not used since the mid-1980s.

Bake Benefits Realization into the Life of a Project
Through a series of discussions during the first meeting, the group concluded that the first task for Kamal was to develop a project plan covering tasks and timing. Kamal agreed, but insisted the group spend more time defining the specific outcomes of the effort they were trying to achieve. While the discussion started slowly and high level, Kamal kept asking questions that helped the group define increasingly specific expected benefits of the effort including a 25% decrease in requests for additional information from industry, and in the number of follow up inspections. Some in the group questioned the value of defining specific targets so early in an effort without any visibility into the issues at hand but eventually the group

agreed that the outcomes would be described as initial targets from which to judge potential changes against.

Bake Post-Implementation Benefits Analysis into the Plan

At the second meeting, Kamal presented his plan to the group, which included mapping current processes, analyzing the processes, developing recommendations, implementation, and refinement. The group heavily debated their charter and whether implementation was even within their scope, let alone refinement. Many in the group felt that implementation was really up to the division's management and they alone were responsible for implementing changes.

In addition, many felt the refinement phase went way beyond their commitment or the purpose of the working group. Those individuals defined the group as nothing more than a recommending body and did not want to be accountable for outcomes that were outside their control to realize.

Kamal agreed that the managers were responsible for implementation but they were indeed accountable for helping improve the processes and that doing this was not a single pass effort. In order to meet management's objective for the group, they had to perform multiple passes on the processes; consisting of at least two analysis, recommendation, refinement iterations. The group was comfortable with the distinction and agreed that the group should at least see the process through a second round of implementation; even if just to report that the organization did not implement the recommended changes.

Use a Maturity Model to Measure and Describe Performance

When the group initiated the mapping activities, they came to the conclusion that in the absence of up to date processes, each inspector had essentially created their own methods for interpreting the procedures. While all inspectors completed the formal checklist and associated forms, the scheduling of inspections was left up to each inspector, some submitted hardcopies while others e-mailed them, and review and follow up was not systematically and centrally tracked making it difficult to for management to achieve any real visibility into activity, status, and workload. The group quickly came to the conclusion that this effort would not simply be about identifying obstacles and opportunities to automate, but would require foundational level activities such as defining and documenting an updated set of standard processes. To demonstrate progress, the group defined a basic maturity model for the effort, defining the current basic policies supported by ad-hoc methods as a level one maturity, and the next desired state as simply having and using a single set of standard procedures for the complete lifecycle. Through a simple set of PowerPoint slides, the group was able to illustrate progress towards this goal.

Conclusion - Using PS Change Techniques

After completing the initial development of updated end to end processes with the goals of reducing requests for information and follow up visits required, Kamal's group worked with the organization's managers to implement them. Initially the inspectors pushed back on the processes due to a number of additional validation steps which added incremental value but appeared redundant. After meeting with the inspectors and collecting feedback from several who tried the new processes, the group refined the processes and identified some basic web technologies that would greatly facilitate the process. After implementing the refinements, the organization was then positioned for the first time in almost twenty years to actually measure the levels of requests and follow up from which to continue to make improvements.

Conclusion - Not Using PS Change Techniques

Using the basic outcomes of increased efficiency and effectiveness, the group developed a basic plan designed to identify improvements. Through discussions with inspectors, the group identified twelve basic recommendations and presented the findings to management. No one followed up to see if any recommendations had been implemented and the organization's managers, with more pressing issues to deal with, moved on to other organizational fires. A year later, a high profile issue in the industry caused the organization's IG to issue a report sighting significantly out of date procedures to which management responded by initiating another effort to review and update the organization's processes.

Projects in the public and private sectors are successfully managed off of cliffs every day. By staying focused on the realization of benefits relative to the level of maturity of whatever the project is focused on, individuals can help an organization drive greater value from its initiatives and projects through better selection and course correction. The act of consistently asking about and focusing on benefits can also help an organization slowly move away from a compliance oriented culture where a significant amount of activity is devoted to answering someone else's mail.

Prototyping

Big projects and initiatives in government generally have low success rates. Even in private sector organizations with deep pockets and committed management, big projects are hard to pull off successfully. In addition, for many government organizations, the pace of external change is already faster than the organization's ability to keep up with it. Just the need to contemplate, review and then re-review plans and ideas internally and externally can represent a significant drag, resulting in projects that simply fall behind the natural pace of the changing world around them.

The common activities associated with any project or effort can generally be illustrated as a pyramid. The foundation of the pyramid represents the planning and analysis activities, where ostensibly the most effort and investment should be made. The middle section of the pyramid represents implementation, construction, or development activities. The top of the pyramid represents the roll-out or go-live of the project and typically represents the point at which benefits begin to be realized.

This approach is very common across many different types of organizations and efforts. However, when an organization spends so much time building the pyramid from the ground up to address a specific objective, by the time the top is reached it's often answering yesterday's problems.

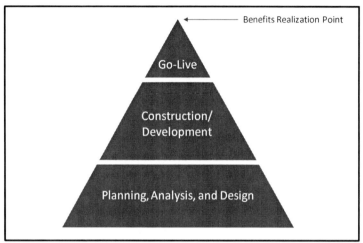

Figure 10: The traditional large-scale effort or initiative with a heavy emphasis on significant planning and analysis.

Time moves on, people move on, things change, and requirements change. So almost by definition when any real drag exists on moving forward, organizations can't embrace this typical approach or they will always be developing solutions and implementing ideas that meet yesterday's problems.

31

Turning the Pyramid
on its Head

Successful efforts in the public sector often take a different approach from the traditional pyramid of plan and action. Instead of the large-scale approach, successful efforts embrace the concept of creating and starting multiple prototypes or pilots on a smaller scale that begin with minimal planning and instead look to implementation and testing as a means for seeing what works.

They essentially shrink the pyramid and turn it upside down. They start by *doing* something, trying different things, and then for those that succeed, step back and start to build more planning and analysis into the prototype that's providing the most benefit. The combination of trying more and different things gives an organization a better shot at finding and implementing something that works.

Rapid prototyping activities in and of themselves are also naturally more collaborative - they generate touch points with the people an effort is trying to benefit and enables it to identify and react to the feedback as well as new information and changes in the environment.

The other benefit of course is that smaller pyramids are more consumable by the organization and simply easier to implement in traditionally rigid environments. So an organization is going to have inherently more success taking any idea and breaking it down into smaller changes.

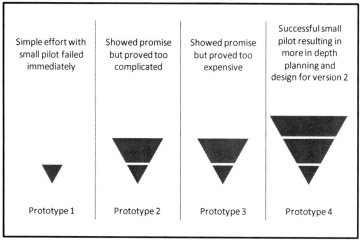

Figure 11: Engaging in multiple smaller efforts enables more innovation and increases the likelihood of finding the right solution that sticks in the organization.

By definition, the large pyramid project is akin to putting all the organization's eggs into one basket. By creating several smaller pyramids with smaller-scale activities, an organization is able to try more things and see what works before making more sizable investments.

32

Piloting Efforts

Moving forward using a pilot approach, a short duration, limited scope implementation regardless of whether multiple efforts are launched provides a number of benefits to public sector organizations. The combination of their limited impact along with the psychological benefit of being perceived as a smaller, potentially temporary change makes their use ideal in public sector organizations.

In many organizations, the lower resistance to pilots relative to changes perceived as more permanent or wide-scale is enormous. People simply tend to react better and accept the concept of pilots more readily; their inherently lower level of risk fits well with the risk averse culture that exists in many government organizations.

The reality is virtually anything can be introduced as a pilot, even large scale changes. Successful change agents in organizations have managed to push through enormous change by disarming the organization by simply labeling the effort a pilot. Certainly if the effort failed to succeed, something else would be done so in essence everything by definition fits in the category of a pilot to some degree.

Beyond a perception standpoint, pilots also often act as a mechanism for sparking innovation. By giving individuals something to react to, it fuels their creative juices and helps them envision even more ways to improve the pilot. They become embedded in the review process which in turn leads to a sense of ownership that occasionally translates into a role of champion of the changes the pilot is seeking to accomplish.

The flip side is that failure to embrace this feedback often leads to the opposite response where individuals reject the pilot because the improvements or changes they identify are never incorporated into the pilot. Incorporating the feedback from individuals represents a great mechanism for securing buy-in to a concept. One federal organization recently deployed a new knowledge management (KM) program to a skeptical workforce using a pilot approach. With little organizational KM capability and a lack of understanding of what to really focus on, the organization launched multiple pilots and solicited feedback. One pilot seemed to almost instantly institutionalize itself across the organization based on the fervor with which the pilot participants used and promoted it. The organization then put more investment into it and similar types of KM capabilities.

33

Phasing Roll-Outs

Another strategy which has proven useful in both the public and private sectors is creating overlaps between the status quo and the changed processes, approach, or technologies so their use and adoption can be phased in. Although not always possible, using this approach allows the changes to be introduced as a test or 'beta' concept which people can embrace if and when desired, followed by a change over at some point where changes become the default while access to the 'legacy' processes or systems is available. Eventually, the legacy environment or practices can be phased out. This allows people to migrate to a changed environment at different paces while lowering transition risk because the legacy capabilities are still available.

The phased approach provides a number of benefits. A Phased effort reduces the risk of transition, enabling smaller segments of resources to try something and provide feedback and ideas not just on the changes but the process of migrating itself. The concept of introducing the changes as a 'beta' also reduces expectations. Labeling the effort as a beta or trial embeds the expectation that not all the kinks may have been worked out and individuals tend to be more forgiving of those kinks. In addition, organizational resistance is lowered and it too is phased as early adopters jump on board, followed by additional adopters which gives the momentum necessary to eventually force the late adopters to move forward.

A federal organization for example recently used this approach to phase in a new set of administrative forms and approval processes. A link was initially provided to the new automated web forms with a 'beta' label encouraging use while the old downloadable forms remained the default option on the web page. After several months the new forms and workflow became the default but a link was maintained providing access for a period of time to the 'legacy' forms if desired. After an additional period of time the legacy link was disabled and eventually the forms were taken offline.

The phased approach can also be used in a more passive way when the ability to dictate change is almost non-existent. Even in environments where no formal control exists to push changes, a new approach, service, or capability can be offered, allowing various organizational elements to leverage it as desired on a 'pull' basis. Over time, through marketing, outreach, and other indirect mechanisms, the changes could become more widely adopted simply because they are superior or proven over time.

Alicia is a Director in a research and science organization responsible for overseeing a number of internal and externally funded research efforts. One of the most common complaints Alicia has heard over the last several years was the difficulty with which information is shared and managed across the organization. Many vendors have presented solutions over time to Alicia and her group, ranging from electronic lab notebook vendors to document and data management software providers.

Each product seemed to offer benefits to the organization but the organization's inability to define its real requirements made it difficult to truly identify the right solution. In some cases, individuals argued for a centralized repository for scientific data and information while others described the real issue as the lack of desire of researchers to share all of their information or findings before it was formally published.

Turn the Pyramid on its Head
Alicia decided, rather than launching a full-scale implementation of any solution, to try several different approaches. She started several pilots of various technologies in order to see which might prove promising within the organization. It soon became clear through several of the pilots that the organization's issues spanned many areas, including a lack of centralized repositories, who

110

would own or be responsible for maintaining the information, and what, if any, information and data standards the organization would embrace.

Pilot Efforts

To manage the efforts, Alicia appointed an individual to sponsor each individual pilot. These individuals were given three tasks to complete within a six month period; identify candidate users for their pilot, ensure use and evaluation of the pilot by the users, and develop and present a short findings presentation on the solution they oversaw.

Users were informed they were simply evaluating new tools to make science and research easier. Alicia was amazed at the level of involvement the users had in the pilot evaluation, becoming either vocal champions or critics of particular solutions.

Phase Rollouts

As a result of the pilots, Alicia narrowed the approach down to the development of an information governance framework coupled with a centralized web-based solution that for the time being would be an optional toolset scientists and researchers could use to share information across the organization. Later Alicia would start to identify ways to store scientific data in the repository that limited its distribution to only those authorized by the submitter of the information.

Conclusion - Using PS Change Techniques

Alicia continued over time to work 'upstream' to leverage the solution and refine the governance model to maximize its value to the organization. The approach proved so successful for Alicia's organization it was used as a model for another agency's approach for managing its data. Alicia's solution and approach was also highlighted at a scientific conference the following year.

Conclusion - Not Using PS Change Techniques

The vendors convinced Alicia that a centralized repository would provide the visibility everyone appeared to desire and certainly the logic of having one was undisputable. After lengthy requirements gathering and design phases, the organization moved forward with the implementation of the repository.

After several months, the repository was populated with a number of data sets but did not seem to contain any useful data despite instructions from leadership to populate the repository with all of the organization's scientific information. After a year, the repository was all but forgotten as the repository was not kept up to date and slowly devolved to the point of being virtually useless to the organization.

Rapid prototyping, pilots, and phased roll-outs offer unique advantages over traditional wholesale efforts. With lower upfront investment and reduced risk, their attributes make them uniquely suited as a major component of many public sector change efforts.

Engineering Discomfort

In the private sector organizational momentum exists naturally through a continual focus on the bottom line, driving companies towards improved effectiveness and efficiency. Whether it's management's constant desire to increase shareholder value, competitive pressures, or the cumulative effect of staff and management reaching for the brass ring, private-sector companies are naturally propelled by individual and collective activities to increase performance.

In the public sector however, those basic motivators are often simply missing. Punitive measures for inaction are often difficult to use and financial motivators are equally limited. Without the ability to fully reward high performance or deal quickly and effectively with poor performance, management is left with an environment where motivators to excel and drive progress are significantly limited. No carrots, no sticks.

The power of praise is effective at an individual level, but moving the collective towards a common goal often requires more significant motivation. In environments lacking traditional motivators or incentives for change, other mechanisms must be used to drive progress.

34

Creating Imperatives

In the general sense, leveraging imperatives as a driver for action represents a useful motivator at the organizational and leadership levels. By consistently conveying that the foundation on which something currently exists is going to come to an end or a highly undesirable event will occur, an organization will likely adopt over time the belief that something must be done.

When executed correctly, it makes doing nothing a non-option. For example, public sector organizations often rely on older technologies where the pain of continuing to maintain and use a system is perceived to be less than the pain of transitioning to something newer. Individuals occasionally leverage the concept of a burning platform in such scenarios by painting the picture of how the old technology will almost certainly fail, perhaps soon, and when it does the parts or expertise to fix it simply won't be highly available which could grind activities to a halt.

In the private sector imperatives are often defined in terms of their focus on value creation. A private sector imperative, for example, is releasing a new product or entering a new market to exploit a niche or keep up with competition. In the public sector, the successful use of imperatives is often focused on identifying and highlighting risk, not opportunity. Developing specific scenarios or vignettes describing the impacts of non-action - public outcry, congressional investigations, lawsuits, an idle workforce – helps make the individuals who need to be influenced or make a decision sense both the potential pain and the organizational and professional risk. The burning platform plays to the heart of a risk averse culture. The more the risk is spelled out, the more effective the concept typically works.

The biggest risk in using imperatives is over or mis-using them. They are a powerful technique but can diminish credibility when used in less than ideal circumstances. In one organization, an individual developed a presentation describing the significant risk and damage the agency would face if it failed to effectively manage the use of Microsoft® Project Server®, a project management software platform. The organization was unconvinced. Imperatives are applied best when real risk, preferably nearer term can be highlighted to motivate individuals into action or decisions.

35

Driving Accountability

At the individual level, more personal motivators are often required. One such motivator for individuals is the use of increased visibility by the organization into an individual's activities. Accomplishing this requires two primary components; assigning explicit activities or performance metrics to an individual and a public forum or mechanism for displaying progress.

For example, creating weekly or bi-weekly meetings where individuals are called on to describe their progress towards goals often generates the appropriate discomfort needed to spur action. People do not want to be seen by their peers or managers as frequently inactive. Repeating this process consistently, providing visibility into the levels of progress or lack thereof, increases discomfort associated with non-action. Few individuals are willing to attend a meeting week after week with peers and management and describe their lack of progress. When leaders state to individuals in meetings, 'we seem to be stuck on this one, when can we expect progress on this?' Individuals will tend to either engage in productive activity or find ways to self-select out.

When performed appropriately and consistently, all individuals in attendance are motivated to make progress before the next meeting. However, this technique should be applied with care. Sugarcoat everything and the anxiety will not be significant enough to drive behavior. Going to the other extreme will destroy the performance culture desired. Over time, the ability to apply this technique with surgical precession will enable the right level of anxiety to motivate action without cutting too deep.

This technique is a general extension of the concept 'what gets measured, gets done.' For example, in an organization that processes documents, publicly ranking the productivity of each individual against their peers creates an almost instant increase in productivity in terms of processing documents. This may mean other things are now not getting done or error rates are increasing, but whatever the spotlight is on, will typically be the emphasis for individuals.

The same approach is also effective in working groups where the group leaders often have no formal management authority over how participants spend their time. Pointing a spotlight on specific activities can be very powerful in a workgroup of a dozen or more people where the progress may be at a trickle. Coupling this technique with time-boxing will often increase the levels of activity significantly.

Another potentially effective mechanism for reducing the natural drag on progress is helping people understand they're not going to run out of things to do - to help them understand they don't need to turn a particular activity into a reason for professional existence. Helping people understand there is always going to be more things to tackle, more ways to drive performance or more requirements to address can reduce their fear that they may not be needed if they 'engineer' themselves out of a job. In organizations that are contemplative by nature the pervading thought is often 'why do we need to rush through this?' The answer of course is that there are other activities that really need to be addressed as well.

The same sentiment often occurs when it comes to automating job functions (people will lose their jobs!). Continuously communicating that there's so much to do, so many higher level activities that need their support, helps individuals accept that there will never be a shortage of things to do. For example, individuals who help automate their previously manual tasks are actually creating an opportunity for themselves to move away from simple task processors to more customer-centric personnel providing higher levels of value to the organization. Over time people begin to accept that progress is not about eliminating jobs, viewing it instead as a way to experience more meaningful careers.

Jeff, a technical project manager for an organization whose primary mission is to provide services to other federal organizations across several agencies, was asked to help the agency migrate its electronic documents from an aging document management system to a modern technical platform. The existing system, while functional, was becoming increasingly expensive to maintain, had slow performance, and lacked many modern features such as robust search capabilities. Jeff read previous business cases which clearly stated the benefits and return on investment from a new platform, but the organization's management seemed unmotivated to move forward with funding the effort or dedicating the resources needed for a successful implementation.

Given the nature of this organization's mission, the impact of slow performance and missing features was virtually impossible to measure. From a personal risk standpoint, leadership was motivated to do little if anything to improve the situation - the risks associated with a complicated systems migration seemed far less than the risks associated with the old system.

Create Imperatives
In order to motivate the organization and its leadership, Jeff developed a list of possible outcomes with their expected probability. The most probable scenario was that

the system would fail, resulting in a complete outage that restricted any access to the data and documents it stored as well as a possible loss of data and documents. The outage would result in an almost complete halt to the organization's activities for an undetermined period of time as well as impacting other agencies, businesses, and the public. Applying basic techniques used to determine impacts from disasters, Jeff summarized the economic, reputation, and other impacts the agency would experience if the system failed. Some leaders pushed back, stating that Jeff could not point to any specific data that would enable him to define the system as out of date or at risk. Jeff provided leaders with vendor documentation which illustrated how the vendors had discontinued formal support and their recommendations to upgrade. Jeff also summarized the risk in obvious terms for leadership stating that 'if we wanted to buy spare parts for the hardware we'd have to get them off eBay and if we wanted to hire a programmer and placed an ad, no one under the age of seventy would apply - it's old and ready to break. Don't be the one who ground several agencies to a halt.'

Drive Accountability

Leadership's decision was to form a working group to assess the need for an upgrade as well as help define a path forward, making Jeff the group's chair. The group spent several meetings discussing the system, debating the merits of an upgrade, and exploring many tangents including the competency of the IT organization and whether it could successfully manage the upgrade. To drive the group in a more productive direction, Jeff began to assign specific activities to most individuals within the group. Initially Jeff would informally ask for updates from people during the meeting and noticed that this attention seemed to drive action in those areas. To take advantage of the effect, Jeff began asking individuals on a rotating basis to present their updates to the group in the form of fifteen minute presentations during each meeting. Over the next three months the group had identified requirements, developed a high-level schedule, and constructed a basic statement of work for use by the agency's acquisition department to procure vendor services to perform the migration.

Conclusion - Using PS Change Techniques

Although it would take another two years to fully complete, the system was successfully upgraded to a modern platform. During the early stages of the migration, the existing system did unexpectedly fail resulting in an outage that spanned several weeks. While the outage resulted in some embarrassment for the agency, their ability to point to their existing effort to modernize the system was equally recognized, significantly mitigating negative perceptions.

Conclusion - Not Using PS Change Techniques

A little more than six months after Jeff's last attempt to garner support the system failed resulting in a several week outage. Although the outage did not cause major disruptions outside the agency, the internal impact on productivity resulted in significant embarrassment to the agency's leadership translating into daily pressure on the organization's IT leadership. Because the internal impact was so wide spread internally and lasted for so long, the CIO and a Division Director were quietly asked to find new positions.

Creating imperatives, when used correctly, act as a significant motivator on an organization and its individuals. When using these techniques, individuals need to be careful they leverage them to define and tailor messages, not to fabricate issues that simply don't exist. If taken too far, individuals run the risk of jeopardizing their otherwise important initiatives while risking damage to their professional reputations.

SECTION 9

Taking Initial Ground Quickly

At first glance, the concept of taking ground quickly may seem at odds with successfully managing the pace of change. However, taking ground quickly is a refinement of the concepts described in earlier chapters. During the initial stages of an effort there is simply less organizational baggage attached, enabling individuals to move quicker. During this early window, activities may be more straightforward to accomplish based on a combination of goodwill and a lack of organized resistance to an effort.

36

Leveraging New Players

New individuals represent a significant opportunity and mechanism for taking ground quickly. Whether joining an organization, a working group, or an effort in any capacity, new individuals typically enjoy the unique benefit of being personally unencumbered by politics and history.

New individuals possess a personal window where they can take ground quickly. Like running into the ocean, these individuals can move fairly quickly at first, as if on wet sand or in a few inches of water. However, as they wade deeper into an organization or effort, their speed slows as the water level rises around their waist. And after a period of time, they're simply treading water to keep their heads above water, merely keeping pace with the operational and compliance requirements of their role. Unencumbered by history, politics, and personalities these individuals possess a good, but diminishing opportunity to make progress.

In one federal organization, the culture placed a high value on the opinions of new individuals, frequently granting them immediate expert status on any given topic. Interestingly, the perception of these individual's opinions changed over time as they slowly but surely came to be viewed as just another individual in the department. In another organization, the viewpoint was the opposite. New individuals were seen as investments, their opinions worth little until they were fully trained in the ways of the organization with few relevant viewpoints because they lacked an understanding of how things 'truly worked here'. The missed value was immeasurable.

New players also possess on a diminishing basis a more objective perspective. Without the history and baggage of why things are the way they are, these individuals have a much better ability to see the 'art of the possible'. Most things in an organization are the way they are for a reason. But often the reason which made sense in the past is simply no longer valid. Requirements change, but public sector organizational structures, roles and processes change in response more slowly. New players offer a form of visibility into what may have made sense, but just doesn't make sense anymore. They are only looking at the current state because it's all they know - what are today's needs and what are we doing to meet them? People ingrained in an organization over time often lack the same ability and perspective to see the gaps as easily. In one organization for example, a new player identified a way to readily reduce the budget planning cycle by months. The current Finance Director was 'aghast' at the thought of changing the process, stating that, "we've always done it this way so why change it?"

37

Where Consultants add Value

One of the biggest values external consultants offer is a fresh perspective. With a hopefully better understanding of the broader possibilities based on experience with many other organizations and efforts, consultants often see the gaps and opportunities between the requirements an organization, program, or project is attempting to address and the mechanisms it's employing to do so.

The value of this external perspective is enormous, but it too diminishes over time. Consultative value often follows a common pattern with some value delivered initially through the introduction of new ideas and the fresh perspective on the organization's activities and approaches. The value peaks as individuals apply that knowledge and insight while leveraging a better understanding of the organization and how things get done internally. During this period, with a developed understanding of the political and organizational structures, processes, and players, good consultants help drive value and make progress towards goals. After a period of time however, that value slowly diminishes as the consultant becomes to some extent viewed as, or even behaves like, part of the organization.

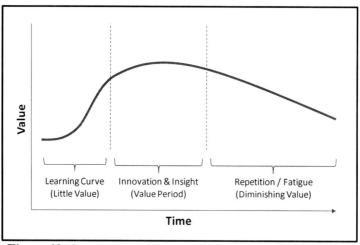

Figure 12: A common value curve for external consultants.

The reduction in consulting value to an organization over time is the result of a combination of factors. One issue is that once a consultant or consulting firm has shared its unique perspective and insights, there simply may not be much more for them to say on a given subject. Few consultants will say the only additional value they can add is to simply repeat what has already been communicated, but this is often the case. If an effort is not moving forward and consulting resources are not transitioning to planning, facilitation or other roles, their overall value drops. In addition, even external resources will succumb over time to the same realities as internal resources and reach a point of simply treading water based on their own accumulated baggage within the organization.

In Bradley's position as an Executive Officer (XO), he was tasked with identifying ways to improve the way intelligence was gathered and consolidated for leadership review. He met with a number of leaders and support staff to gather a combination of requirements and ideas on how to improve information collection and reporting.

Leverage New Players
One of the leaders Bradley spoke to had just joined the organization. This individual described to Bradley his initial impressions of the reports, identifying potential improvements to the synthesis and analysis processes, report formats, and reporting frequency. Through the discussion Bradley was able to see the end to end process in a whole new light. The individual identified new data sources as well as ways of combining information Bradley and no one else in the organization had ever considered. The individual also questioned the value of many reports, describing many as irrelevant to the issues at hand. Bradley began to realize that the reports were at one time relevant but while time moved on, the reports had simply never changed.

Leverage Consultants the Same Way
To support the development of new reports and reporting processes, Bradley issued a task to an existing vendor to help with planning and implementation. After reviewing the

objectives and requirements, the vendor showed Bradley how another organization had implemented a customizable but still formatted report functionality which married the benefits of pre-formatted reports with ad-hoc reporting capability. The vendor continued to offer good ideas as the process went on until the new reporting capabilities were implemented. However, Bradley noticed that the vendor was providing new ideas on a less frequent basis over time and the impact and scale of the ideas were diminishing over time as well. Ultimately, Bradley introduced a new vendor to keep the effort energized.

Conclusion - Using PS Change Techniques

By leveraging a resource new to the organization, Bradley was able to deliver true innovation through the initiative. The leadership was able to use the more relevant information to readily address current issues and opportunities. In addition, by leveraging multiple vendors over time, Bradley was able to inject innovation and energy into the effort for a longer period of time.

Conclusion - Not Using PS Change Techniques

After learning the leader was new to the organization, Bradley elected not to talk with him in order to avoid having to invest the time and energy explaining to the individual how the organization worked. Bradley talked to other leaders who described their challenges but didn't gain much insight into what kinds of data would provide the insight they sought. In the end, Bradley reached out to a vendor to perform an assessment which resulted in a new reporting tool that added some flexibility and value but overall the effort was described by one leader as 'old wine in a new bottle'.

Don't miss early opportunities to accelerate efforts before the effort picks up too much baggage. By accelerating what is feasible early and taking advantage of new or external resources for their unique windows of insight, efforts have the opportunity to pick up much needed steam early in their life, setting the foundation for long but well established efforts.

Making Working Groups Work

A lack of vision and clear objectives is often blamed for many failed public sector initiatives. Certainly having a vision is an important component of any effort, but often the blame lies in too much visioning relative to execution. The ability to successfully move past visioning and analysis activities and into execution represents a significant factor in getting things done in the public sector.

38

Developing Visioning Tracks

In highly inclusive environments, initiatives and projects will often include a combination of individuals who lack a material understanding of all the dimensions of what is being considered as well as those who simply want to contemplate and discuss things but have little impulse to do much more. The initial education of these individuals serves a useful purpose as initiatives get underway, helping the larger collective learn various dimensions of the problems or opportunities under discussion. The time comes however when action is required, and these same individuals and their desire to continue to 'understand' and 'evaluate' become roadblocks to progress.

Acknowledging that some may never truly be comfortable participating in a decision, efforts may need a separate track or work-stream for these individuals so that they can continue contemplation while others move forward with execution activities. The goal of the visioning track is to essentially provide individuals with a distinct role which serves the dual purpose of continuing visioning but also takes them out of the hair of individuals trying to move forward with getting something done in the nearer term. One working group leader for example, after her group focused on updating policies failed to make progress after several months, developed a 'road show' activity for a member who kept arguing heatedly with other members at every meeting. Once this member was deployed on a cross-country effort to spread the word, the group began to make immediate progress towards publishing revised policies. In another organization, several members of a working group who slowed every meeting to a crawl with endless philosophical questions were tasked with creating background and informational content to support the effort which required a separate set of meetings focused on that activity. The frequency of the group's main meetings requiring their attendance was then reduced.

By acknowledging that some individuals will simply be drawn to continuous contemplation, giving them the ability to spend their time on visioning as long as they desire without attempting to force its conclusion will enable others to move forward at an accelerated pace with the execution of identified opportunities.

39

Turning Working Groups into Programs

In any organization, there are many types of groups, ranging in formality, size, and duration. At one end of the continuum, there are ad hoc groups that may assemble over a single lunch to address a very limited issue, such as how to fix a software bug. At the other end of the continuum are formal organizational components such as a division branch, with a formal structure and activities designed to endure indefinitely.

Working groups, with their informal structure, often fall closer to the ad hoc end of the spectrum. This is often appropriate to address very simple issues or initiatives but has significant weaknesses for initiatives with broader scope; efforts that require significant planning, analysis, project management components, or substantial change.

Most working groups in the government tend to be single-threaded; that is, everyone in a group is contemplating and discussing the same thing at the same time. However, analyzing the nature and structure of an envisioned or current working group against its objectives represents a significant factor in the group's eventual success. When the wrong structure is applied, the group may lack the organization necessary to effectively address larger issues or in the case of simpler objectives, may be weighed down by structure and organization resulting in an equal lack of progress towards straightforward recommendations.

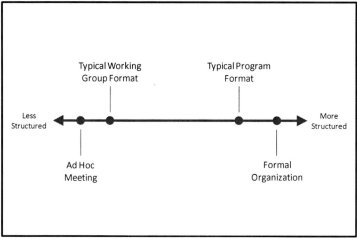

Figure 13: The spectrum of groups commonly found within an organization and where working groups typically fall within that spectrum.

In order to successfully decouple those who desire continuous contemplation from execution activities, to successfully 'divide and conquer' and move forward faster, an individual may have to develop sub-groups within a working group where individuals focus on different things and report back to the larger working group on a periodic basis. This change shifts the standard working group closer to a program structure, which is often a better fit for many initiatives addressed by working groups.

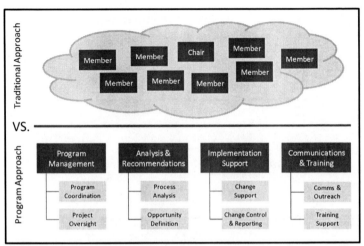

Figure 14: The traditional working group approach versus the program-structured working group approach.

With resources deployed across a broad range of areas in a more execution-oriented way, more gets done faster and better. The very structure drives a mental shift within a group from being contemplation-oriented to execution or implementation focused.

To address the presence of individuals who lack a desire to move past contemplation, make at least one program segment's activities focus on continuous visioning, analysis, and communication activities. These activities may never end, but as good ideas emerge from and around these activities, individuals in one sub-group can focus on their implementation while the other continues to refine the associated messages.

40

Time-Boxing Activities

Another important concept for managing within the structure of working groups is placing limits on the time spent on any given topic and assigning due dates to action items. This concept, known as time-boxing, can act as a significant accelerator for efforts, especially those with open-ended objectives. The best efforts possess a macro level time-box for the complete effort. Within that time-box, smaller segments of activity are also time-boxed to help ensure they are accomplished within the overall timeframe of the larger effort.

One area of time-boxing that sometimes limits its use is difficulty determining how much time is the 'right' amount of time for a given segment of activity or area of focus. Many efforts will begin by assessing the relative importance of each activity to the overall effort and then assigning more time to more important activities and less time to less critical ones.

Time-boxing also embeds a powerful concept into its very structure, the concept of diminishing returns. For many segments of efforts, the best ideas and most effective progress will come early on, and time-boxing represents a mechanism for moving on before specific efforts extend too far past their value. Even when time-boxing is used as a looser concept, it typically acts as a motivator for concluding activities closer to the timeframe originally envisioned and moving on to other areas of activity.

Time-boxing also acts as a mechanism to diffuse a real risk in any working group: the desire to get everything 'exactly right' before moving forward. The desire to define perfection before moving forward has derailed a significant number of otherwise well-meaning efforts. Many efforts begin with an over-arching objective to identify the 'best' outcome or end state. The problem is in most situations, there is no actual 'best'; the optimal outcome or end state is more likely the result of a series of trade-offs between concepts such as cost and benefit or risk and reward.

The concept of perfection is essentially a paradox. The usual result of trying to define the absolute ideal is a series of looping discussions that typically fail to arrive at a universally accepted conclusion - passionate discussion followed by little or no action. More importantly, sufficient information may not even be available to determine an ideal balance until some level of implementation occurs which provides better information or visibility into the problem or opportunity. Instead of spending cycles searching for nirvana, successful efforts typically start by identifying components of a better foundation, moving forward with implementation as rapidly as possible, and adjusting over time.

This, of course, is harder than it sounds. In rigid organizations with poor decision-making capabilities, establishing a baseline capability instead of studying a problem for an extended period and coming up with the perfect answer may be untenable. Few solutions, if any, may have been implemented on a temporary basis historically because change is so hard to accomplish in the first place, therefore resistance exists to doing anything without significant contemplation and getting it 'right' before execution. Time-boxing places a limit that helps force decision points with regard to objectives, recommendations, or solution structures, helping to keep efforts from falling into the perfection paradox.

41

The Value of Good Facilitation

Many working groups leverage external facilitators to help move efforts forward. The use of external facilitation can be an important accelerator, helping facilitate a variety of activities, from brainstorming to achieving consensus around various concepts. Ideally the facilitators, whether it's one or multiple individuals, possess an appropriate level of depth in the subject matter, good change management skills, and a good understanding of the organization, its culture, and political environment.

The facilitation role, when performed by a truly experienced individual, represents a powerful support mechanism for moving efforts forward. Unfortunately, many organizations and working group leaders underestimate the value of highly experienced facilitators; instead viewing the role as more of an administrative one. In fact many public sector organizations acquire facilitation expertise through the same administrative contracts and organizations that provide other services such as event planning and recording meeting minutes. The use of less experienced facilitators represents at a minimum a missed opportunity. In worse cases, they may actually inhibit progress by facilitating the wrong things - trying to reach complete consensus, failing to time box activities, or attempting to define perfect solutions for example.

Some of the best facilitators really don't describe themselves by that title; instead they see themselves simply as subject matter experts, consultants, or in some cases, professional coaches. Regardless of title or source, the ability to find and leverage a high quality, experienced individual in a facilitation role can be a significant accelerator for those using working groups to address issues or opportunities.

Marie, a section chief for a small independent agency, was asked to lead a new working group charged with evaluating ways to improve one of the agency's grant programs. The program is generally viewed as effective but its administrative costs have steadily increased over several years. To maximize the identification of potential improvements and ensure consensus, leadership included working group members from several offices including the CFO's office, the acquisition office, the office of program assessment, the IT group, and the grants office itself.

Although the group's diversity was intended to add value, the membership's lack of understanding of the grant program's purpose, and for some, the purpose of grants in general, translated into several initial extended sessions focused on simply educating the group about the program. Basic sessions were eventually replaced with more in depth discussions about the program's operations that were resulting in higher spending on its management. After six weekly meetings the group had still not had a chance to discuss potential improvements. Several of the group's members were ready to move on but other individuals wanted to continue studying the role of federal grants in private sector markets while other working group members were insisting on 'going back to basics' and collecting requirements through focus groups and surveys in order to re-engineer the program from scratch based on requirements.

Develop Visioning Tracks

It became clear to Marie about six weeks into the working group's existence that several individuals simply weren't ready to move on to discuss existing suggestions for improvement and instead continued to want to share new insights they were discovering about the program or its grant recipients. To move the effort forward, Marie developed an outline for the group's deliverable, hoping the blank document would start to generate a bit of anxiety in the group to help them focus on addressing the task at hand. After contemplating the different areas of the document different members could address, Marie decided to divide the document's sections among the team, asking several individuals who seemed more interested in examination than action to address the background sections that described the role of the group, its goals, and the purpose of the grants. After dividing the tasks, Marie discovered that by directing the individuals who seemed to be slowing the group down on these specific tasks, the rest of the group found it easier to begin assessing identified improvements.

Turn workgroups into programs

After the group had developed, evaluated, and prioritized a list of proposed improvements, the organization's leadership asked the group to oversee their implementation. To better manage the group, Marie divided the group's activities and resources into three sub-teams, one focused on overall planning and project management, one focused on implementation activities, and one focused on communications and outreach. The implementation team helped the program implement actual changes such as updating process documentation and getting IT resources to add functionality such as converting several paper processes to online forms with workflow. Their efforts were supported by the project management group's plan development and the communication group's slide decks explaining the changes and their intended benefits. Weekly one hour meetings kept each team on track with short updates on activities performed and planned provided by each team.

Time box everything

Leveraging the plans and the interrelated and dependent activities of each sub team, Marie constantly communicated the deadlines for each team relative to the others' activities in order to lower the risk of any team falling behind. Marie also set limits on review time of anything another group produced to two days. Although some questioned the need to limit reviews, instead arguing for more thorough vetting across larger groups of people, Marie described larger cycle deadlines, such as the upcoming grant competitions combined with downstream activities that would need to be performed to further emphasize the need to move as fast as possible with the current activities.

Marie also consistently emphasized timing and deadlines in each meeting to keep the group time-aware with regard to any activities. Over the months, the constant emphasis on timing and deadlines became a standard part of any discussions about required activities.

The value of facilitation

To support the group's activities, Marie requested the use of contractor support and facilitation from the organization's leadership. Initially, the organization provided an in-house facilitator to support the group's efforts, but Marie found the facilitator seemed to be more interested in enabling philosophical discussion. Instead Marie transitioned the facilitation to a contractor resource that had started his career in the federal government but had moved into the private sector. The individual significantly accelerated the conversations and quickly helped the group identify and refine its ideas and plans.

Conclusion - Using PS Change Techniques

Over the course of nine months Marie's group was able to implement several changes in the grants program focused primarily on converting most of the paper-based process steps to online distribution and capturing reviews online. The result was a decrease in contractor administrative support by 50% in the first review cycle. The changes also helped identify additional changes to the program slated for implementation after the current grant cycle ended. Marie and the members of the workgroup received an award for their support in helping the group realize the reduction in the percentage of overhead relative to the total grant pool.

Conclusion - Not Using PS Change Techniques

Marie's group met for six months continuously discussing the opportunities resulting in the development of a PowerPoint presentation describing potential changes to the program's approach. While many of the recommendations were useful, it remained unclear how the recommendations would be implemented and who was responsible for executing the changes. The next two competitions proceeded in similar fashion to previous years' competitions.

The frequently elusive goal of working groups is balancing the value of collective thought with the natural drag created by the inclusion of larger groups of individuals in the process. By structuring working group activities, developing visioning tracks, leveraging techniques such as time-boxing, and using high quality facilitation the overall value of working groups is improved while minimizing its limitations.

Maximizing the Value of Consultants

The value of external consulting resources can play a vital role in the success of projects and change efforts within the government. They also commonly add little value, and in some cases hold efforts back with poor advice.

Let's briefly look at the typical consulting engagement lifecycle. The default starting point for many consulting engagements is an assessment of the current state. An assessment can prove helpful, but many organizations have already completed one or possibly several assessments of a particular subject or function over a period of years. The consultants dutifully identify their mechanisms for collecting information, such as interviews and surveys, complete the results and report out the findings. The assessment typically takes weeks or months to complete but unless this is the first such assessment, the real value is often the education of the consultants, not the client - they are now at least up to speed on the organization and its challenges.

The next phase is typically the development of potential solutions. This effort may add more value, depending on the experience and capability of the consultants, but often times only results in a list of previously known options.

Only at this point, after the investment of perhaps the majority of time and money under a given task, do the consultants come to realize the same thing the organization already inherently understood: it's not 'what' needs to be done, but 'how' to get it done that the organization really needs help with. How to adopt and adapt; to change.

42

Consulting Versus Real Experience

Good consultants understand the 'what' versus 'how' issues in the government. Through a combination of hands-on experience and understanding of the tenets of being a trusted advisor, good consultants provide deeper insights through better instincts to their clients. They're practical, they understand how to deal with complex issues, and they tell it like it is.

At the other end of the spectrum, consultants whose total professional experience consists of 'consulting' experience only truly know one thing: The business of consulting. These individuals specialize in applying and executing a methodology to a problem set; in assessing, analyzing, and recommending based on what the method tells them to do. Without any real experience in the underlying job functions, they often miss the subtleties, realities, and practicalities of the client's actual environment. The use of these resources can work, but consultants with real experiences who work collaboratively with clients simply work better.

Let's look at an example from this book. A consultant is asked to facilitate a working group. Does the consultant with little or no practical experience pull the chairperson of the group aside after a period of time and say, 'I think we're going in circles here, have you considered bifurcating the group to some degree to enable progress?' More often than not, the group will receive from this type of support very clean meeting minutes, and timely status reports showing a 'green' dashboard because the contract is burning as expected. The consultant with real organizational and operational experience however advises the chair based on a combination of the goals of the group and the realities of its ability to make real progress.

Another good example is an effort to identify savings or efficiencies in a functional area. The consultant with experience limited simply to consulting can successfully execute a data collection process which may collect ideas from individuals in the organization through interviews or even conduct a benchmarking study where ideas are collected from other organizations. But a consultant with real experience already possesses a wealth of ideas, can better identify new ones, and better assess the value and feasibility of options for the organization based on their past experience of actually knowing what works.

Good federal leaders understand this dynamic and often work to structure contracts not to get the best firms, but to get the best people from any firm. They often look at a potential contract based on the quality of the team and the resources as a significant differentiator over the soundness of a proposed methodology or approach.

43

The Real Value of
Tools and Methodologies

A common selling point for many consultancies and contractors are in fact their unique or specialized methodologies and tools. What one often finds under closer inspection of these methods however, is that the vast majority of them are fairly similar to a handful of almost universally common approaches. One firm's specialized methods for example, as published on their website under different service areas, are actually all the same approach with only a handful of words changed and the color scheme altered within each one.

A firm's methodologies are often touted as a differentiator and certainly possessing a consistent approach is better than having none at all. But for many firms, the methodology, and the extensive training that firm's provide their consultants in the methodology represent an inadvertent mechanism for institutionalizing mediocrity. They represent a device to eliminate spectacular failures but occasionally displace intellect and common sense in unskilled consultants. On one project for example, a firm's consultants provided the client with a draft list of interview questions for identifying areas to cut costs. It was clear almost immediately that the template was from the firm's toolkit and included a significant number of questions that were unrelated to the effort. The firm's consultants were essentially asking the client to apply the intellectual capital and expertise to the effort.

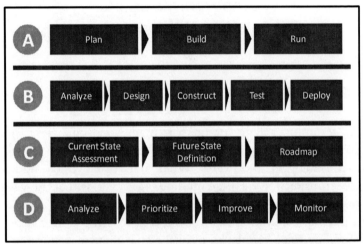

Figure 15: Examples of universal approaches that sit at the heart of many specialized and highly touted methodologies.

Pre-defined methodologies are helpful, but the best firms and consultants recognize them for what they really are - a starting point. They represent mechanisms that help guide and accelerate efforts but if applied without customization by unskilled practitioners in a public sector environment, they typically result in minimal actual progress. A canned method applied by a general resource often misses the art within the science of change, the subtle course corrections required on an almost daily basis to guide efforts successfully forward.

44

The Weaknesses of Benchmarking

A common mechanism for identifying opportunities for improvement within public sector organizations is the use of benchmarking. Usually performed by external firms, benchmarking involves selecting a number of areas of an organization for examination and comparing their practices, approaches, and outcomes to one or more similar organizations.

Ideally, the benchmarking effort results in a list of fully vetted and mature ideas ready for implementation. The reality is that benchmarking in the public sector typically results in few if any meaningful opportunities. In many cases, public sector organizations are truly unique with specialized missions, needs, and operations with few if any similar organizations. In other cases, the benchmark targets are comprised of other public sector organizations with the same sets of systemic or cultural challenges. After one federal organization for example completed a bench-marking study of their practices against other federal agencies, the project sponsor declared, "I thought we were bad, but I actually feel better about the way we do it here now."

Another issue for public sector organizations associated with benchmarking is the lack of value in comparative quantitative data. The ability to define and compare equal metrics is often difficult and the root cause of what is driving the results of the metric is almost impossible to pinpoint in a short benchmarking effort. At best, typical benchmarking efforts often only reveal very high level trends that pinpoint areas for additional review.

The highest value of benchmarking however is often not in the quantitative or qualitative comparison between organizations or their activities, which is what many consultancies originally set out to capture. The true value lies in the cross-organizational dialogue that often takes place during the benchmarking effort. To capitalize on that value, many benchmarking efforts emphasize not similarity but differentiation in the targets. The goal of the effort is not about an apples to apples comparison, but an exposure to the 'art of the possible' from a wider variety of organizations. This type of benchmarking is not about comparing metrics but about comparing ideas for the purposes of sparking innovation. Organizational leadership that compares for example their human capital practices to a local cable content provider often stands more to gain than comparing their practices to a similar government organization. What they find won't be a seamless fit but will often provide substantially more ideas to contemplate, evaluate, and implement.

45

Finding Client-Focused
Service Providers

Another important element driving the value of external services firms is how they define their own purpose. Many public sector contracting organizations define themselves not by the value they add, but by their ability to simply capture revenue from the federal competitive contracting process. They view the market not as a challenging environment requiring top shelf talent to solve some of the most complex problems in the world, but as an ATM machine requiring no more than the right code to extract money. These organizations exploit the government's natural and inherent acquisition and related weaknesses for their own gain, providing services and personnel which offer little or no value.

One mechanism for identifying whether a vendor is focused on adding value is whether they actually say they can't do something or tell the client about a firm that does something better than their own firm. Organizations and consultants that do this are typically demonstrating a higher level interest in the client's success. Those that consistently say they can and do provide every kind of service the government is seeking are often focused on revenue rather than client value. A client once remarked in a meeting to a small firm, after they declared over the course of the meeting that they could support eight totally different projects, "You have five employees, you guys are really the best firm in all of these areas?"

Recognizing organizations where even meeting with a potential client and understanding their challenges is not in their business model is an important element in predicting what types of support those organizations are truly going to provide. One organization, which was eventually debarred from federal contracting for failure to consistently perform, actually created software designed to process government requests for proposals which spit out a draft canned response by taking all sentences in a statement of work and adding the words 'we will' in front of each one. Firms, on the other hand, that demonstrate not just a willingness but a desire to understand a client's organization and mission typically apply the same level of desire and focus when delivering services.

Organizations with a true client value purpose and a desire to add specific values in particular areas, tend to represent significantly better support options. They attract and retain better talent, deliver more specific services more effectively, and perhaps most importantly, acknowledge the limits of their role and look for new challenges rather than ride the consulting value curve beyond its logical conclusion.

Marcy, coming off a successful project, was put in charge of her organization's newly created program management office (PMO) responsible for overseeing nine different but related projects. One of Marcy's first activities was to establish a contract to deliver support services to the PMO.

Consulting versus Real Experience

At the contract kick-off, Marcy met two of the contractor's key personnel, Leon and Sharon. Sharon had joined the firm right out of school eight years ago while Leon had spent the first ten years of his career working directly in areas the projects were focused on. Sharon and Leon worked with Marcy for the first couple weeks establishing plans and developing processes for tracking progress, costs, risks, and other project related information. Although helpful, after the initial efforts Sharon was only able to collect and convey information provided directly by the project teams. Through his previous knowledge of the areas, Leon was able to work with each team to fully identify and assess risks, identify opportunities to improve the solutions being implemented, and work with the team to identify ways to overcome a variety of obstacles.

The Real Value of Methodologies and other Tools

One of the selling points for the contractor selected to support Marcy was their PMO methodology and toolkit. Although the firm's methods and tools were helpful, they didn't quite fit the nature of the efforts Marcy was responsible for. Recognizing this, Leon modified the templates the firm traditionally used to better meet Marcy's needs. Leon also dropped several unnecessary activities from his firm's approach based on information he received during the beginning of the project.

Purpose Driven Organizations

One of the first projects the team reviewed and worked with was an effort focused on the development of a website used for industry filings to the agency. The project had an initial budget of $300,000 which both Marcy and Leon agreed seemed high relative to the straightforward requirements. But the project was more than nine months behind schedule and its budget had been amended three times to now over $1M. The company responsible for implementing the site had an excuse for everything, blaming the agency for changing requirements and its inability to provide timely feedback. Marcy's review of the effort showed that the contractor was billing for its people eight hours per day even when the ball was almost exclusively in the government's court. During discussions between the contractor and Marcy, the contractor seemed completely un-phased by the situation, telling Marcy that this was typical of software development efforts and Marcy was simply not experienced enough to understand the technical issues.

Marcy asked another organization to perform a review of the technical project. The review indicated not only that the original $300,000 was high, but that the agency already had a working site for another purpose that it could readily adapt for minimal investment.

Conclusion - Using PS Change Techniques

Marcy convinced the organization to abandon the current implementation effort and initiate a new project to adapt the existing capability. Because of contractual realities, the same failing organization was tasked with the effort. However, Marcy and her team closely monitored the activities and project metrics and the new effort was successfully completed.

Conclusion - Not Using PS Change Techniques

The PMO support firm provided Marcy with a number of individuals with little real experience that attempted to apply their firm's PMO framework and methodology to Marcy's PMO without modification. The result was a significant amount of time and energy performing unnecessary activities, re-performing activities that had already been completed by others, developing a large number of reports and dashboards for leadership, and implementing a robust but expensive project management portfolio system. After a few months, the realities of several of the failing projects began to impact the organization's stakeholders including one high-profile failure after go-live. Because Marcy's organization was created to prevent just this scenario, and the PMO itself had to increase its budget already, Marcy was viewed largely as the individual most accountable. While she argued that more resources were necessary (the contractor was unsurprisingly supporting this same conclusion), Marcy was replaced with another PMO lead and put on a rotation to an unrelated organization.

Simply put, individuals with real experience will always offer greater value than individuals whose sole experience is consulting. In addition, organizations that put their clients before profits will always deliver greater value than organizations which provide whatever services the client is looking for in order to drive revenue. An individual's ability to secure their services from these resources and firms will have a significant advantage over those that use lower quality resources from firms focused solely on revenue captured as the measure of success.

Knowing When To Move On

A common view of many efforts and initiatives is that they are unsuccessful if unfinished. Certainly a half-built facility or only parts of a missile add little value until they're completed. But with change efforts, this typical view is often misleading. If structured properly, focused on direction and adding incremental benefit along the way, change efforts are often best concluded before all possible value has been extracted from the effort.

46

Diminishing Returns

Many change efforts reach a point where continued investment or effort simply exceeds the likely benefit. Whether its internal obstacles or simply unpredicted issues, the best course of action is often to conclude an effort and declare victory even if additional value is theoretically possible. Using an effort where consolidation of something is the goal for example, consolidating down to one of that something may be the ideal. However, fewer of that something may be all that is realistically possible. To continue to invest beyond 'fewer' to try to get to 'one' may simply not be worth the effort required in many cases.

In some cases the cost in the cost/benefit analysis is dollars - such as when a simple spreadsheet may prove to be almost as effective as a more substantial database application. In other cases however, the cost may be an individual's own political capital or reputation which is better saved for accomplishing something else instead of more from the same effort. In other cases, it's simply the opportunity cost - time spent trying to further improve the accuracy of reporting for example may be better spent tackling a completely different problem. This is where the perfection paradox often comes in - good is often good enough when other priorities, crises, and requirements beg for attention.

Setting expectations upfront regarding the point of diminished returns is also important to ensure the organization and its leadership views the progress for what it is, a success, rather than viewing the lack of reaching nirvana as a failure. In one agency for example, a working group spent over a year trying to define an organization-wide data taxonomy. At first the effort moved smoothly with the major aspects of what the organization did fitting nicely into an easily agreeable structure. But as time moved on and the group dove deeper into the details, the effort ground to a halt as almost no one would agree on compromising their sub-categorizations that they had built their organizations around over decades. In the end the group produced a nice document but the proposed changes were never accepted or implemented and the effort's intended benefits were never realized. An almost identical taxonomy effort took place at another agency but the group, recognizing that it was unfeasible for every organization to change their information paradigm overnight, quickly switched gears to implementing a new top level structure in their organization's document management system. The new top-level categorization was applauded for bringing 'order to chaos' within the agency's system.

47

Knowing When to Quit

A closely related concept to diminishing returns is simply knowing when, organizationally or otherwise, no successful scenario exists. If there are no combination of moves that enable a win, stopping the effort is the winning move.

Often however, stopping an effort itself can prove difficult in public sector organizations. The effort may already be funded and supported by contracts or the organization's leadership won't accept that the effort is not viable or doesn't want to deal with the political fallout associated with stopping the effort. If the organization and its leadership can't be convinced to focus the investment of time and money on other opportunities, individuals may have to extract themselves to focus on other things if something can't be stopped or re-directed, handing responsibility for continuation of the project off to others until they or a combination of people and events convince leadership to wind it down. Going down with the proverbial ship may be noble, but getting more things done is a better use of time.

The opposite phenomenon can play out as well where an individual may be asked to take over a failing effort. In these cases, the individual needs to examine the 'opportunity' closely to determine whether a successful outcome is possible before jumping on board. For example, an organization recently brought in a consulting firm to help a new project manager turn around a failing project. It turned out that this new project manager was the third project manager in eighteen months to take the reins of this effort. He, like his predecessor had been told (sold) that they had the capabilities to right the ship. In actuality, each of the previous project managers, recognizing that the effort was doomed for a number of reasons were looking to put the ticking bomb in someone else's hands. With support from the consulting firm and both the previous project managers, the project manager was finally able to convince leadership to quietly wind down the effort, effectively diffusing the bomb.

In some cases, the issue is not the viability of the idea or effort, but that it's simply the wrong time in the organization's maturity for it. Good ideas and activities are often mis-timed relative to the organization's ability to adopt or leverage them. A service catalog may be perfect for an IT group for example, but if it hasn't yet embraced the concept that it's a service organization, the service catalog concept is unlikely to succeed in that environment. In these cases, if helping the IT group evolve isn't an option, moving on to other things is often the right approach.

Scott, a facilities manager at a federal agency, has just been tasked with helping his agency refresh its Continuity of Operations Plan (COOP). To move the effort forward, Scott helped the organization identify the impacts of potential outages and disasters. Next Scott identified alternatives the agency could use to mitigate outages and fail-over to redundant operating capacity in the event of a disaster. The next step for Scott was the development of the COOP itself, the objective of which was to document the steps necessary to recover from an outage or disaster.

Scott's efforts moved forward in a fairly straightforward manner until he completed his alternatives analysis. Although Scott had no trouble identifying impacts and assessing alternatives, he found it much harder to get management to agree to actually fund and implement the fail-over capabilities. Despite agreeing with his findings, the agency's leadership seemed unconcerned with the gaps his analysis identified between the agencies requirements and its capabilities.

Diminishing Returns
His management asked him to move forward with the development of the plan regardless because the agency was required to create and maintain one. Scott tried to point out that the plan actually provided no benefit unless the fail-over investments and capabilities it described actually

existed. Scott's management agreed with the basic dilemma but asked Scott to address the gap as best he could. In the plan itself, Scott addressed what he could but left the components of the plan that documented the steps associated with the non-existent capability at a very high level.

Sometimes Folding is the Right Move

Figuring little value was derived by going into depth documenting capabilities that didn't actually exist and would likely be different than imagined once implemented, Scott buttoned up the document and moved on to other efforts. Scott decided if and when the agency did invest in the fail-over capability, he would revisit the plan.

Conclusion - Using PS Change Techniques

Scott's organization ended up with the best plan it could develop given its actual capabilities. When the plan was reviewed as part of a controls review, the gaps were formally noted giving Scott more ammunition to get the agency's leadership to make investments in the area. In the meantime, Scott used his time to help the IT organization focus on identifying ways to mitigate more localized outages by better configuring the data center facility.

Conclusion - Not Using PS Change Techniques

Scott expended significant effort trying to document the details of a fail-over and restoration of agency services based on capabilities that were not yet in place. After several months of trying, Scott contracted out the plan development. After considerable effort, the agency eventually invested in a fail-over capability but the components of its approach were radically different from the developed plan. Based on the changes in its actual approach, the existing plan offered little value and plan development was again contracted out and completed in order to align the current plan with reality.

It's often difficult to know when to end efforts in the public sector. This difficulty stems from the unique nature of change efforts in government where the finish line isn't always clear. Improving things' or making things more 'effective and efficient' also creates a very difficult to define finish line. There's often no winning score, no switch that gets flipped, or even a timer that reaches zero. If an effort possesses definitive goals, an individual has to reasonably try to accomplish them. But for those that don't or can't be reached, in order to stay effective, individuals must develop an ability to almost sense when the value equation between investment and return peaks; and at that moment move on to the next challenge.

CLOSING THOUGHTS

Views of the public sector's value vary wildly across America. On one end of the spectrum, some see it as one of our nation's greatest strengths while others view it largely as an unwarranted expense of tax dollars and borrowed debt. These views often trickle down to individual perspectives of the nation's public sector workforce. Regardless of political orientation or perspectives on its broader value, the reality remains that getting things done in government is not easy. Its characteristics and culture place enormous professional burdens on the individuals who have dedicated their lives to serving the public. Finding ways to change it and ways to make progress requires a combination of passion and perseverance which represent the true motivators that replace in the public sector the concept of profit-seeking in the private sector.

Similarly, individuals who focus on consulting to the public sector are sometimes viewed as less skilled than their commercially-oriented counterparts. The logic goes that if they were better at their craft, why would they not be commanding higher rates from commercial clients? In practice however, these individuals are actually some of the most talented in their fields - the best possess the ability to help organizations move forward in the face of tremendous challenges like nothing that exists in the private sector.

Even though the average public sector worker or consultant is unlikely to make wholesale changes to the way government fundamentally works, if armed with the tools to succeed in making smaller changes, the opportunity exists to add incremental value while changing, ever so slightly, the culture and direction of the enormous vessel that is our nation's government. With enough individuals focused on incremental change and progress in renewing and refreshing the approaches of our government, the opportunity exists to drive broader change from the ground up - to make larger scale progress through thousands of smaller but meaningful successes.

About the Author

As an operational leader, management consultant, and trusted advisor for over eighteen years, Patrick Chapman has helped dozens of public and private sector organizations improve performance, reduce costs, and realize true value from change.

As founder of Make Government Better, (www.makegovbetter.org), Mr. Chapman is currently working to identify new ways to bring ideas and innovation to federal agencies.

CPSIA information can be obtained at www.ICGtesting.com
Printed in the USA
BVOW031400191211

278730BV00007B/30/P